Presented To:

_____

From:

_____

Date:

_____

The 40 DAY
Soul Fast

The 40 DAY Soul Fast

Your Journey to Authentic Living

DR. CINDY TRIMM

DESTINY IMAGE® PUBLISHERS, INC.
P.O. Box 310, Shippensburg, PA 17257-0310
"Promoting Inspired Lives."

This book and all other Destiny Image, Revival Press, MercyPlace, Fresh Bread, Destiny Image Fiction, and Treasure House books are available at Christian bookstores and distributors worldwide.

For a U.S. bookstore nearest you, call 1-800-722-6774.
For more information on foreign distributors, call 717-532-3040.
Reach us on the Internet: www.destinyimage.com.

ISBN 13 TP: 978-0-7684-4026-3

ISBN 13 Ebook: 978-0-7684-8872-2

For Worldwide Distribution, Printed in the U.S.A.

8 9 10 11 12 13 14 / 17 16 15 14 13

And what do you benefit if you gain the whole world but lose your own soul? Is anything worth more than your soul.

—Jesus

(Matthew 16:26 NLT)

Contents

Section I:
Journeying Toward Authenticity

Section II:
The 40 Day Soul Fast

Week One:
The Power of Forty:Enlarging Your Capacity

Week Two:
The Purpose of a Soul Fast:
The Self-Leadership Challenge

Week Three:
The Nature of the Soul: The Essence of You

Week Four:
The Properties of Thought: You Are What You Think

Week Five:
The Importance of Identity:
Becoming a Master by Mastering Your Mind

Week Six:
The Power of Words: Healing the Hole in Your Soul

Week Seven:
The Power of Doing: God's Chosen Fast

Week Eight:
Sealing the Healing: The Cleansing Power of Love

Foreword

T.D. Jakes

Though man has traversed the earth, built the most impressive buildings to protect himself from its often unforgiving elements, climbed the most foreboding mountains, fought the greatest battles, defied the most devastating natural disasters, harnessed electricity, broke the sound barrier, unveiled the secrets of the atom, captured and transmitted images and sound from continent to continent, healed diseases with a pill, destroyed viruses with an invisible beam, and fired rockets into outer space we are still on a quest to find answers to life's mysteries. If he would but read the Bible, he would discover that the answers he seeks can actually be found much closer to home—God has locked them up within his soul; for there, He has placed eternity (Eccl 3:11).

The soul, housing the mind, will and emotions, is truly the last great, unexplored realm on earth. Its fertile soil is enriched with divine substance, which is far more precious than all the wealth in the world. What does it really profit us if we gain the whole world and lose our souls—the essence of who we really are? This fertile field of unlimited potentiality must be excavated, explored, and cultivated so that its full potential can be realized.

You hold in your hand a tool that that is designed to do just that. It has been written with the view of transforming your inner life so that you can truly live authentically. When people hear the world fast, the first thing that usually comes to mind is abstinence from food. Jesus said, "It is not what goes in a man that defiles him, but what comes out." I have discovered that all of us need to detox our "inner man" from negativity, carnality, and the memories of past hurts and pain, which act like a virus in our mind and a cancer within our soul.

God can use this 40-day fast to break down and eradicate spiritual contaminates and launch you into a deeper walk with Him—a life of true freedom and happiness. I believe this is a very timely book—one that will equip you to discover, and in some instances rediscover, who God intended you to be as you unearth the rich deposits he has placed deep within the inner chambers of your spirit.

We all have those moments in our lives when we need to stop and take stock of those things we harbor in our soul that should be discarded. Very few of us actually take the time to do this. As a result, our truest self becomes buried under the weight of unforgiveness, doubt, fear, hurt, betrayal, rejection, and disappointment. Life's challenges have so many of us living our lives in a state of chronic stress. It's time to de-stress.

I believe that the Church is in the beginning stages of the greatest revival this world has ever known. In order for us to carry out the plan of God, we must realize the life-changing power of living authentically—living inside out. We must revolutionize our world by stepping into the fullness of God's perfect, unique plan placed within each individual. Instead of conforming to the world's expectations, we must boldly walk in the fullness Christ provided by living from our deepest, most honest selves.

In a time when many people are trying to find out who they are, this book will challenge you to get to know who God truly designed you to be and equip you to maintain your originality.

There can be copies, look-a-likes, sound-a-likes, and duplicates, but never another original you. If you sometimes feel you are not fully using your strengths and talents, or that your work is no longer meaningful or challenging, you may be facing a crossroads.

This may be a time of uncertainty and fear, but also a great opportunity to move forward in a more satisfying direction. You may be in the midst of restructuring your life after a bout with illness, a job loss, or trying to find meaning and purpose as you reenter the workforce, or even trying to find stability after a divorce.

You may be at a crossroads in your personal, emotional, or spiritual life. Wherever you find yourself, this book will help you to assess your current state of being—including your goals, values, attitudes, behaviors, character, and desires—and give you a spiritual compass of truth that will help you to proceed purposefully and congruently with God's will and plan for you.

When you live according to His will and Word, the result is personal wellness, career success, ministerial vibrancy, and increased effectiveness in your relationships. Dr. Trimm refers to this concept as "Living Authentically" and effectively shares how to walk that out day-to-day.

If you have a personal relationship with God, you have a calling on your life. God may want you to be a pastor, an evangelist, or a missionary. He may want others to be a light in the business world. The hand of God may be upon you to write books, discover a cure for some deadly disease, feed the hungry, provide shelter for the homeless, lead people into a place of safety and hope, or raise godly children.

Gifts and callings were not placed in your life to lie dormant. They are God's best for you, and only by yielding to His Spirit working in and through you will you see them fulfilled. This book will guide you; transforming how you live so that you can meet challenges, overcome self-defeating habits, maximize your full potential, and release your anointing.

Dr. Cindy Trimm is a profound and prolific communicator of truth. She walks you through this 40-day journey step-by-step. If you apply the 40 characteristics of an authentic person to your daily life, you will begin to experience a new freshness in God. This book will make your heart sing and your soul rejoice. The plans that you have hoped to fulfill all your life will come to fruition. Do you long for the deeper things of God? Does your soul stir at the thought of doing exploits on His behalf? This sense of destiny will cause you to determine that no matter what you must face, you can and will fulfill God's best for your life!

This powerful *40 Day Soul Fast* will take you to higher heights and deeper depths in God. Get ready to spend the best 40 days of your life, experience a new joy and power that will change you from the inside out—and position you to positively influence the lives of those around you!

You will discover that when you live authentically, you will see yourself as God sees you. You will develop a renewed sense of wellbeing, balance, and peace. When you are true to who you are, walking out your destiny, fulfilling your purpose, and giving from a whole and healed place—offering the best of yourself in service—you will make this world a better place.

Foreword

If I could summarize this book in one sentence, it would be: You were born an original; don't live a life as a poor replica of someone else. Live authentically.

Bishop T.D. Jakes
Senior Pastor
The Potter's House of Dallas, Inc.

The most desperate need of men today is not a new vaccine for any disease, or a new religion, or a new "way of life." Man does not need to go to the moon or other solar systems. He does not require bigger and better bombs and missiles...His real need, his most terrible need, is for someone to listen to him, not as a "patient," but as a human soul.

—TAYLOR CALDWEL

Quick Start Guide

Joining the Movement

Begin to see yourself as a soul with a body rather than a body with a soul. —Wayne Dyer

Capacity building by learning to live authentically is what *The 40 Day Soul Fast* is all about. Capacity building, in a way, is also about community building. It's about growing into "the fullness of God" as a community (see Eph. 3 and 4). Don't journey alone! There is power in community. There is strength in numbers. I challenge you to bring at least four friends along with you on this soul-healing adventure

If everyone who picks up this book takes it upon him or herself to encourage four other people to participate, we would create an unstoppable movement! You may think that one healed soul cannot heal the world, but it can.

If you would like to bring healing to your community, nation, or hemisphere—or if you would like to see positive change even closer—in your home, your family, church, or organization, please consider doing the following:

1. Give your pastor, group facilitator, or community leader a copy of the book.

2. Identify and promote the long-term benefits of soul healing.

3. Get *The 40 Day Soul Fast* program on the agenda and calendar!

4. Start a signup sheet. Pass around a clipboard asking interested individuals to sign up.

5. Start your own small group that meets weekly for the next eight weeks.

6. Find all the tools you need to become a soul fast leader online at www.soulfast.com.

7. Order books in larger quantities at a discount.

8. Buy two extra copies and share with two of your closest colleagues, family members, or friends.

9. Discover your AQ! Find out your Authenticity Quotient by taking the free AQ Assessment at www.soulfast.com.

For more information about how to facilitate a *40 Day Soul Fast* in any setting, please visit www.soulfast.com. Every one of us can make a difference. Together, we can heal the world.

I am personally convinced that one person can be a change catalyst, a "transformer" in any situation, any organization. Such an individual is yeast that can leaven an entire loaf. It requires vision, initiative, patience, respect, persistence, courage, and faith to be a transforming leader. —Steven Covey

Is not this the kind of fasting I have chosen: to loose the chains of injustice and untie the cords of the yoke, to set the oppressed free and break every yoke? (Isaiah 58:6 NIV)

Preface

For Freedom!

To deprive a man of his natural liberty...is starvation of the soul. —Mohandas Gandhi

I am so glad you have chosen to join me on this 40-day journey to greater mental, emotional, and spiritual health! If you are looking to transform your life, you are in the right place! Over the next eight weeks, I will teach you the foundational principles of spiritual and personal empowerment—no matter what your background or experience, you will learn and grow and be empowered like never before to maximize your personal potential and break through to greater success.

My heart's cry is to liberate the souls of humanity so people everywhere would be empowered to grow into their most authentic, God-created, divine selves. Of course, it is only through a personal relationship with your Creator that you can truly be set free. As St. Augustine once said of the Lord, "You have made us for Yourself, and our hearts are restless until they rest in Thee."[1]

Throughout the next 40 days, we will be talking a great deal about entering into that rest, what it means, and how it can empower us to live more authentically. We will be stopping to look around as we are told in Jeremiah, *"Stop at the crossroads and look around. Ask for the old, godly way, and walk in it. Travel its path, and you will find rest for your souls..."* (Jer. 6:16 NLT). And as Jesus so gently implored, *"Let Me teach you, because I am humble and gentle at heart, and you will find rest for your souls"* (Matt. 11:29 NLT).

This *40 Day Soul Fast* is about finding rest and restoration for your soul. When all is well with the souls of humanity, all will be well in the world. When you have peace in your soul, you will bring that peace to bear on the world around you—you will become the change you are hoping to see.

A prayer offered by the Rev. Noelle Damico, a respected clergywoman and activist who has coordinated fasting campaigns for social change, echoes my prayer for you as you begin this 40-day journey:

> May this fast be a time of purification for you, as you seek truth and clarity. May it be a time of divine encounter, when you experience the presence and power of God. …May it be a time of re-orientation that you may name the patterns of injustice and commit anew to their transformation. …Together, may we be the change we wish to see in the world.[2]

May we all feel the presence of God each and every day as we *"do our best to enter that rest"* (Heb. 4:11 NLT). And as we take up residence there, may we become more acquainted with our authentic selves and equipped to walk in the light of what we discover.

> Be your authentic self. Your authentic self is who you are when you have no fear of judgment, or before the world starts pushing you around and telling you who you're supposed to be. Your fictional self is who you are when you have a social mask on to please everyone else. Give yourself permission to be your authentic self. —Dr. Phil McGraw

> *For freedom Christ has set us free; stand firm therefore, and do not submit again to a yoke of slavery* (Galatians 5:1 ESV).

SECTION I

JOURNEYING TOWARD AUTHENTICITY

Chapter One

A Series of Unfortunate Events?

There is no chance, no destiny, no fate, that can circumvent or hinder or control the firm resolve of a determined soul. —Ella Wheeler Wilcox

Have you ever had a feeling that something is holding you back? Have you ever wanted to do something different, be someone greater, or go somewhere you've never been, but you don't because of one reason or another? What trips you up? What is it that keeps you from being your best self and living your best life filled with joy, peace, and happiness? What could it be that is holding you back, weighing you down, and keeping you from forging ahead and achieving your goals? Is it your environment, your circumstances, or is it *you*? Could things be the way they are because you are the way you are? Has your success been hindered by a series of unfortunate events—or could it actually be a series of unfortunate decisions?

If you picked up this book, you are among the few "courageous souls" bold enough to take a deeper look into their lives and face some potentially painful and maybe even embarrassing—yet liberating—truths. Too many cruise through life unwilling to read the signs posted along the way. "No matter who you are, no matter where you live, and no matter how many people are chasing you, what you don't read is often as important as what you do read," wrote Lemony Snicket, the author of A Series of Unfortunate Events. Snicket opens chapter one of book seven in his series with this extremely insightful concept. "For instance," he continues, "if you are walking in the mountains, and you don't read the sign that says, 'Beware of Cliff' because you are busy reading a joke book instead, you may suddenly find yourself walking on air rather than on a sturdy bed of rocks."[1] I am reminded of David's resolute prayer in Psalms:

> *Barricade the road that goes Nowhere; grace me with Your clear revelation. I choose the true road to Somewhere; I post Your road signs at every curve and corner. I grasp and cling to whatever You tell me…I'll run the course You lay out for me if You'll just show me how* (Psalm 119:29-32).

David knew there was no better signage available on the road of life than God's Word. The above verse is preceded by, *"Build me up again by Your Word"* (Ps. 119:28). Most people, even believing Christians, don't give the Word of God much mind. They go through life so engrossed and pre-occupied with what is convenient that they miss what is truly valuable and necessary—and as a result, they stay on the road going nowhere, building their life on air rather than on a sturdy bed of rocks. Jesus taught: *"Whoever hears these sayings of Mine, and does them, I will liken him to a wise man who built his house on the rock"* (Matt. 7:24 NKJV). *"Like a man…who dug deep and laid the foundation on the rock"* (Luke 6:48 NKJV). This is what I have written this book to help you do—to dig deep and build the foundation of your life on the sturdy bedrock of your most authentic self.

What is your true north—the plumb line of your soul? I want to help you navigate your own heart's compass and accurately read the signs posted along the way so you don't find yourself running in place with no ground underneath you—or as Paul wrote, *"uncertainly (without definite aim)…like one beating the air"* (1 Cor. 9:26 AMP). I want to help you *"Run to win!"* in life (1 Cor. 9:24 NLT).

Some of the most prevalent and misunderstood things that keep people from running with purpose and certainty are the toxic thoughts and lethal strongholds within their souls—memories of painful experiences, destructive habits, emotional attachments, misplaced desires, limiting beliefs, and narrow objectives undermine purpose, meaning, and lasting fulfillment. Unaddressed, these things will cause you to go through life feeling weighed down. Unidentified, such things will continuously burden your soul, and sometimes take the wind right out of your sails so you find yourself floating a drift with no shoreline in sight. Now more than ever, at this time in history, God's people must *"lay aside every weight, and the sin which so easily ensnares us, and let us run with endurance the race that is set before us"* (Heb. 12:1 NKJV).

The weights that tie you down not only make you vulnerable to sin, but also cause you to acquire maladaptive sets of behaviors that keep you stagnated and going around in circles. These patterns derail you from fulfilling your dreams and cause you to abort your purpose so eventually you leave this earth never fully realizing your potential. Not only that, but when you are unable to break free, you keep those around you bound up as well. You become part of the problem rather than the solution. You join the ranks of blind leading the blind. Jesus asked His disciples, *"Can the blind lead the blind? Will they not both fall into the ditch?"* (Luke 6:39 NKJV). You become the hurting who hurts and the disappointed who disappoints.

There are apartments in the soul which have a glorious outlook; from whose windows you can see across the river of death, and into the shining city beyond;

29

but how often are these neglected for the lower ones, which have earthward-looking windows. —Henry Ward Beecher

There seems to be little awareness of what over time has formed the framework for the paradigms that dictate how people walk out their lives spiritually, culturally, morally, socially, and institutionally. You must be brave enough to ask yourself, "Why do I do the things that I do?" "Why do I keep attracting the people I really do not want and repelling the people I do?" "How can I break negative cycles?" "How can I grow spiritually and do something great for God within my lifetime?" The Bible says when you ask a question, you will get an answer. (See James 1:5.)

In my years of observing people, it has become glaringly apparent that most folks are generally oblivious to how their decisions and thought patterns affect those with whom they interact on a daily basis, and vice versa—let alone how every-day words and decisions affect their own destiny. This is heart—wrenching to me. Time and again I've heard the cry of people who have been deeply hurt or negatively affected by the words or actions of another. If you listen carefully, you can hear the desperate pleas of people crying out for help from emotionally desolate places —it may be a silent cry not demonstrated by tears, but by a seething undercurrent of rage, anger, bitterness, withdrawal, isolation, jealousy, hatred, manipulation, or random emotional outbursts, all masked by a peculiarly unsettling silence. It is not so much about what they are eating naturally speaking, but what is eating away at them spiritually and emotionally. All actions or reactions not born of love are simply a cry from deep within—a cry for healing and freedom—a desperate plea to be freed from the weights and bondages that bind a soul to continual defeat, failure, and despair.

Sadly, many of us are so self-absorbed we have become deaf and desensitized to the cries of others who long for the same freedom and relief that we do. Perhaps we, being imprisoned in our minds, are unable to help anyone else simply because we lack the ability to help ourselves. Like ravenous wolves, we furiously pursue the objects of our own immediate needs and desires, descending upon the bleeding hearts, bruised spirits, and scarred souls of others to satisfy our own needs unaware or unconcerned that there is a silent sufferer in our midst. This is nothing new. We can see in Scripture that when the Israelites had no judge—no moral or ethical accountability, no mentor, standard-bearer, spiritual deliverer, or vision-ary leader—they did what was right in their own eyes. They became self-promoting, self-justifying, and self-indulgent in an effort to artificially appease their aching souls that had become separated from God. In their wake was left a desolate carnage of souls, spiritually and emotionally massacred. The sinking ship of society's morals—and morale—takes all pas-sengers down with it.

Have you ever had a sinking feeling in your soul? Have you ever felt as if you were drowning in loneliness, anxiety, uncertainty, hurt, fear—afraid to trust again, afraid to love again, emotionally bankrupt, or like something had a spiri-tual lien on your soul? Have you ever felt the overwhelming waves of depression crashing against your mind, or, when you take one step forward you end up having to take two steps backward? If the answer is "yes" to any of these questions, then I believe the next 40 days could be the best 40 days of your life.

Where you are now is a direct result of every decision you have made in the past. In other words, the life you are liv-ing today—the state of your relationships, the joy and peace you are experiencing, or the sorrow and pain—finds its root in decisions you have made up until this present moment. Your life is simply a representation of the sum total of your choices—choices that either enslave or save your soul. Think about that for a moment. Ultimately, you are only one decision away from changing everything. One decision can change the trajectory of your life.

My highest calling and greatest reward in life is launching you into a new level of victorious and joyous living by establishing you in the knowledge of the truth of God's Kingdom—knowledge that will set you free regardless of the unfortunate events, decisions, or relationships you've been bound by in the past. Jesus promised His disciples, *"You will know the truth, and the truth will set you free"* (John 8:32 NIV). The truth will set the *real* you—the divinely created you that has been held captive—free from the limitations of your unsaved, enslaved soul! Let's get started unlocking the real you!

> The power for authentic leadership, Havel tells us, is found not in external arrangements but in the human heart. Authentic leaders in every setting—from families to nation-states—aim at liberating the heart, their own and others', so that its powers can liberate the world. —Parker Palmer

> *Embrace this kingdom life and don't doubt God, you'll not only do minor feats like I did...but also triumph over huge obstacles* (Matthew 21:21).

Chapter Two

Twenty-one Grams

The soul is placed in the body like a rough diamond, and must be polished, or the luster of it will never appear. —Daniel Defoe

In 1907, Dr. Duncan MacDougall of Haverhill, Massachusetts claimed to have discovered that the human soul consisted of material substance. Through his laboratory work, he determined that this substance could not only be weighed, but also measured. Through a series of experiments, Dr. MacDougall discovered the human soul on average weighs approximately 21 grams—just less than an ounce. How did he come to this conclusion? Quite simply. As it was understood that the soul left the body upon death, he weighed his human subjects just prior to their dying and in the moments just after they passed. It was ascertained that upon death, the standard amount of weight lost by each of these subjects was 21 grams—whereas when he weighed various animals under the same circumstances, no weight loss was measured. Although Dr. MacDougall's findings were never taken seriously by the scientific community of his day, more sophisticated measurement tools and electromagnetic detection devices have caused his theory to become more widely accepted.

Today, it is believed the average person loses closer to two ounces when they die. Some scholars attribute this loss to what many have defined as a person's "electromagnetic life force," which is strictly unique to the human species. Therefore, when we are referring to the human soul, we are talking about a measurable substance that has been scientifically proven to exist.

This substance is what gives each person his or her distinctive identity, personality, mental faculties, talents, emotions, and will. It is where we derive our sense of self and individuality. In the words of Ray Charles, "What is soul? *It's like electricity—* we don't really know what it is, but it's a force that can light a room." Our soul determines everything about who we are, from our appetites to our ambitions. It is our life force that leaves an indelible mark on all we meet—we may forget a face, but it is a person's soul that leaves the most lasting impression.

> The human soul is God's treasury, out of which he coins unspeakable riches. —Henry Ward Beecher

From the beginning, God set humankind apart from the rest of creation by breathing into the first man His very own breath and causing him to become a living soul—an eternal, thinking, feeling, rational, creative being like Himself.[1] He created humankind in His own tripartite image[2]—spirit, soul, and body. The Trinity of the Godhead is comprised of God the Father, God the Son, and God the Holy Ghost.[3] When we are born into the family of God, His DNA is activated within us—His Spirit comes alive within our spirits, we are given the mind of Christ, and every cell of our mortal bodies is revitalized by the power of His resurrection life. Every aspect of the Godhead comes alive in our own tripartite being—His Spirit comes to live in our hearts,[4] His Nature takes up residence in our consciousness,[5] and even His eternal Word is made flesh in our mortal bodies.[6]

So why doesn't every believer in Christ walk in complete victory in all areas of their lives? Why do God's people struggle generation after generation, day after day, not only with the multitude of opposing forces at work in the world, but the forces at work in their own minds and bodies—even in their own souls? The great apostle Paul wrote about this very thing in his letter to the Romans, *"But there is another power within me that is at war with my mind. This power makes me a slave to the sin that is still within me"* (Rom. 7:23 NLT). What is this enslaving power? Paul admitted that this power *"makes me a prisoner of sin that controls everything I do"* (CEV). How can you be a child of God and still a slave of sin?

THE SOUL OF THE MATTER

Your soul is comprised of your mind, your will, and your emotions. The soul is the seat of one's intelligence, conscience, and reason. That soul is contained within a physical body that God created from the dust of the earth—a body created from the earth to interact with and function in the physical realm. With the aid of five physical senses, the body enables humans to be conscious of the world around them giving them the ability to discern earthly things. In contrast, the spirit of humanity was created to reflect the image and likeness of God, making us *God-conscious* and giving us the ability to interact with and discern spiritual things. So while the body is temporal and Earth-bound, the spirit is eternal and Heaven-bound. These two planes of existence—the earthly and the heavenly—come together in the human soul. The great battles taking place between the kingdoms of Heaven and Earth—between the kingdom of darkness and the Kingdom of Light—are for the souls of humanity. These battles not only rage *in* our souls, but *for* our souls.

The soul, in essence, is where the temporal and eternal aspects of human existence intersect. The soul gives human beings the ability to discern the divine self—to be self-aware—and to consciously live a life elevated by the Kingdom of God while still physically bound to the Earth. The soul is the seat of intention, conscience, and choice. In other words, the soul is the governing mechanism of your life, which in turn is either governed by Christ, the world, or the enemy. What you allow to govern your soul is what you have tethered it to. Is your soul governed by the love of money or the love of God? What do you hope and long for?

Hope acts like an anchor that will either tether your soul to the Kingdom of God or to the kingdoms of this world—to your painful past or to the promise of your future. Paul told the Colossians, *"The lines of purpose in your lives never grow slack, tightly tied as they are to your future in heaven, kept taut by hope"* (Col. 1:5). It is our hope in God alone that provides *"a strong and trustworthy anchor for our souls"* (Heb. 6:19 NLT).

As we talk about all the snares and insidious attachments that can anchor or tie your soul to ungodly and even destructive elements, I want you to remember that hoping in God will always reconnect and anchor you to His saving grace. This hope will purify you, as the apostle John wrote, *"Everyone who has this hope in Him purifies himself"* (1 John 3:3 NKJV)—and it will detoxify your soul. Hope in Christ—your *"hope of glory"* (Col. 1:27 NKJV)—will clear away the impurities and cause your best, most authentic self to come forth.

> I am only one, but I am one. I can't do everything, but I can do something. The something I ought to do, I can do. And by the grace of God, I will. —Edward Everett Hale

> *We throw open our doors to God and discover at the same moment that He has already thrown open His door to us. We find ourselves standing where we always hoped we might stand—out in the wide-open spaces of God's grace and glory, standing tall and shouting our praise (Romans 5:2).*

Chapter Three

Soul-Man

Just as a mirror, which reflects all things, is set in its own container, so too the rational soul is placed in the fragile container of the body. In this way, the body is governed in its earthly life by the soul, and the soul contemplates heavenly things through faith. —Hildegard of Binden

The word *soul* comes from the Hebrew word *nephesh*, which when translated generally refers to a "breathing, thinking being with passion, appetite, and emotion." According to *The Hebrew-English Lexicon*, it literally means the "complete life of a being" defined by the following characteristics:

1) soul, self, life, person, being, mind, consciousness, desire, emotion, passion, appetite

   a) that which breathes, the breathing substance or being, the inner being of man

   b) living being

   c) living being (with life in the blood)

   d) self, person, or individual

   e) seat of the appetites

   f) seat of emotions and passions

   g) activity of the mind

h) activity of the will

i) activity of the character.[1]

The soul is the driving force that causes a person to dream. It gives a person the power to imagine a desired outcome and the determination to complete a goal. It provides the motivation, willpower, desire, drive, enterprise, passion, resolve, urge, and zeal to accomplish an objective. The soul gives a person the mental faculty to make decisions including judgment, discernment, discretion, volition, prudence, judiciousness, discrimination, conviction, belief, and faith. The soul endows a person with the ability to think and apply knowledge via the intellect, understanding, creative power, sensibility, wisdom, and intuition. The soul empowers a person to perform a task by providing an individual with ability, potential, aptitude, competence, capacity, facility, skill, and wherewithal. The soul, which sets humans apart from every other created being on the Earth, is governed by an individual's will and unique patterns and processes of thought—divinely ordained and comprised of a person's temperament, personality, proclivities, mindset, disposition, destiny, and purpose.

The soul gives us a sense of individualism so that we can distinguish ourselves from other souls, as well as a sense of obligation that connects us during moments when demands, concerns, and even threats compel us to take action on behalf of others. The soul is designed in such a way that when healthy and unencumbered, it filters out what is bad or inappropriate and allows in what is good and wholesome. It is for all of these reasons that I find the science of the soul so fascinating. What is it about an individual soul that makes it especially resilient—or particularly vulnerable?

The highest and most profitable learning is this: that a man have a truthful knowledge and a full despairing of himself. —Thomas à Kempis

How is it that one kind of stimuli imprisons one person yet liberates someone else? How does one personality captivate one individual and yet repulse another? Are we predisposed to follow a certain path in life, or are we simply products of our environment? Can we really live a liberated life? Can our souls really be set free? The apostle Paul wrote, *"Christ has set us free to live a free life. So take your stand! Never again let anyone put a harness of slavery on you"* (Gal. 5:1). Paul continues to talk about what it means to be truly free—and how the world system enslaves us by feeding the insatiable beast of our selfish nature.[2] *"My counsel is this,"* Paul says, *"Live freely, animated and motivated by God's Spirit"* (Gal. 5:16). Why? Because this is the very reason why Christ died on the Cross. *"Jesus...offered Himself in exchange for everyone held captive by sin, **to set them all free**"* (1 Tim. 2:4).

It is absolutely clear that God has called you to a free life. Just make sure that you don't use this freedom as an excuse to do whatever you want to do and destroy your freedom. Rather, use your freedom to serve one another in love; that's how freedom grows. For everything we know about God's Word is summed up in a single sentence: Love others as you love yourself. That's an act of true freedom (Galatians 5:13-14).

I believe "true freedom" is the soul state to which God has been striving to return us. God, the Master Creator, created you and I for freedom and good works—and *"He who has begun a good work in you will complete it"* (Phil. 1:6 NKJV). God said, *"My purpose will be established, and I will accomplish all My good pleasure...truly I have spoken; truly I will bring it to pass. I have planned it, surely I will do it"* (Isa. 46:10-11 NASB). God is the *"author and finisher of our faith"* (Heb. 12:2 NKJV). We know from the Book of Jeremiah that the soul of an individual is formed by God before it ever manifests in the Earth realm at a precise time for an exact purpose: *"Before I formed you in the womb I knew you, before you were born I sanctified you,"* (Jer. 1:5 NKJV). God told Jeremiah, *"I know the plans I have for you...They are plans for good and not for disaster, to give you a future and a hope"* (Jer. 29:11 NLT).

But even Jeremiah struggled to embrace his destiny because of what he believed in his soul about himself. His self-perception did not line up with God's perception of what he was capable of. He believed lies that entangled his soul in self-doubt, fear, and shame. God's cure was to put His life-affirming, kingdom-dominating words into Jeremiah's mouth.

> *Behold, I have put My words in your mouth. See, I have this day set you over the nations and over the kingdoms, to root out and to pull down, to destroy and to throw down, to build and to plant* (Jeremiah 1:9-10 NKJV).

Just like Jeremiah, we must put God's words in our mouths about who He says we are. As a first century writer, Publilius Syrus stated, "Speech is the mirror of the soul; as a man speaks, so he is." Everything that comes out of our mouths affects the life of our souls. If you want to position yourself differently and posture yourself for success, then you must *speak* differently.

I remember watching a movie called *Soul Man*. It was about a white man who wanted to understand what it felt like to be black. Instead of asking for an explanation, he sought to experience it by emerging himself into the world of color. His experience spoke greater volumes than someone telling him. He crossed over in order to understand. He simply "became" what it was he wanted to know more about—someone other than who he had originally been—and although it was awkward at first, he walked in this new pair of boots until they fit naturally and became comfortable. He got *soul*.

In our own way, we are each soul-people seeking to understand a world outside of ourselves—a world we are born into while at the same time called out of (see John 17)—a world that is at odds with our most authentic selves. How do we go against the grain—swim upstream so to speak—and learn to live more authentically? We must practice. And then we must practice some more, until our own authenticity—the Spirit of God in us—becomes the governing force in our lives. We must put on Christ and wear that kingly robe of righteousness until it feels as natural and comfortable as an old pair of boots (see Gal. 3:27; Isa. 61:10).

> I believe that man will not merely endure. He will prevail. He is immortal, not because he alone among creatures has an inexhaustible voice, but because he has a soul, a spirit capable of compassion and sacrifice and endurance. —William Faulkner

✳ ✳ *Receive with meekness the implanted word, which is able to save your souls* (James 1:21 NKJV).

Chapter Four

Learning to Live Authentically

The accusation that we've lost our soul resonates with a very modern concern about authenticity.
—Patricia Hewitt

I am on a mission to reconnect you with the true essence of a healthy soul—to lead you to a place in God where your soul can be healed—to reacquaint you with your authentic self. The next 40 days of getting to know the real you are going to be the best 40 days of your life! More importantly, when you learn to live authentically, from a healed, whole soul, no leaks, no punctures, no wounds—free and clear from artificial, socially modified, cultural toxins—you will not only change your life, you will be poised to change the world.

I believe that strengthening people at the level of their soul—restoring the soul and establishing it as the core and essence of who they really are as self-directed people of value, intelligence, and greatness—will change the world. We must break the false perception that as individuals what we do does not make a difference in the greater scheme of things. We are as a nation, as a people, nothing more than the sum of our parts. As the giant world-changer, a small man by the name of Mohandas Gandhi, once said, "A nation's culture resides in the hearts and in the soul of its people." We will only be as whole and healed as a country as we are as a people.

The purpose of this *40 Day Soul Fast* is to not only bring health and restoration to the souls of individuals, but also to provide a mechanism for every person to learn to live from the inside out—from their authentic, God-nature selves. The goal of this 40-day journey is to guide you through the process of discovering who you really are, assist you in the examination of all your objectives and relationships, and thrust you onto a new path of achievement and abundance. I believe that as each person learns to live more authentically, they will not only live more purposeful and fulfilling lives, but as a result, will affect the world for good.

The Rev. Noelle Damico calls fasting a "spiritually and socially transforming practice." She states, "Fasting helps us identify the grave injustices around us, acknowledge and take responsibility for our participation and complicity in such injustice, and prepares us to act with God to transform ourselves and our world." This is at the heart of why I feel this soul fast is so important. It helps us get to the root of who we are and what we represent. This practice is for the purpose of drawing us closer to our own potential by cutting through the clutter and noise of the world swirling around and within us—to help us settle our souls so we can hear from our own hearts—to incline our ears to hear the heart of God beating within ours. Carl Jung said, "Your vision will become clear only when you look into your heart." This is the voice of your authentic self.

Soul-living pioneer (founder of SoulLiving.com) Valerie Rickel sums up the power and significance of living authentically as "creating and living your highest purpose."

> There is nothing more important or meaningful in life than honoring your authentic self—your true nature—and expressing it in the world. When you honor your most authentic self...you are allowing your light to shine and touch the world. Living authentically, in its simplest terms, is living your truth, the truth in your heart and soul. It's allowing

yourself to be guided by Divine Truth and Wisdom each and every day, and doing your highest, most authentic work in the world. It's joyfully creating and living your highest purpose![1]

Imagine how the world would change if every person did their "highest, most authentic work"—imagine a world inhabited by purpose-driven people operating in higher dimensions of love, empathic understanding, and community—people empowered to change their communities, schools, systems, and institutions—people who have found their voice and dare to use it. There is nothing more dangerous than a disempowered person, let alone a disempowered society. Learning to live authentically is about empowerment.

Live your beliefs and you can turn the world around.
—Henry David Thoreau

THE POWER OF AUTHENTICITY

So what does authenticity mean in the context of your life? A common definition of *authenticity* used in the field of psychology refers to the attempt to live one's life "according to the needs of one's inner being, rather than the demands of society or one's early conditioning...authenticity is the degree to which one is true to ones own personality, spirit, or character, despite [external] pressures."[2]

Dealing with these external pressures—the demands of other people close to you or society in general—can leave you feeling conflicted, lost, disconnected, empty, or worse, scarred. I think of the pressure used to mold something into a shape that afterwards looks nothing like the original form. If God is the one doing the molding, this can be a wonderful and beautiful thing, but if it's a corrupt world, forcing you into a false mold never intended by your Maker, it can be debilitating.

The purpose of the soul fast is to help you break free from the soul-constricting pressures and minutia that have held you back and kept you from living a more abundant and authentic life. As with any fast, you want to eliminate those things that deter you from being led of the Spirit—with the soul fast in particular, we are looking to eliminate whatever might derail you from fulfilling your purpose and living your best life possible. As Socrates said so long ago, "The unexamined life is not worth living."

More important than purging toxic lies from our souls is nourishing them with the truth. Not only do we want to eliminate destructive mindsets by fasting from negative, life-sapping thought patterns, but we want to create new habits by feasting on positive, life-enhancing truths about who God says we truly are—truths that will nurture and cultivate our divine, authentic selves.

This is why I have identified what I believe are the 40 characteristics of an authentic person. For the next 40 days, we will be learning about the 40 characteristics you can foster to help undergird and strengthen your authentic self. Throughout this process, you will be asked to journal about what is keeping you from fully embracing each characteristic or living it out more fully in your daily life. By identifying those things that only you—with the help of the Holy Spirit—can pinpoint, you can begin to eliminate the little foxes and extra weights that perhaps you were never aware of before.

We will focus on cultivating one characteristic each day in order to feed and strengthen your soul with the overall purpose of empowering you to take every thought captive until your life is *"shaped by Christ."* I like *The Message* translation of how Paul explains this process in his letter to the Romans:

> *So here's what I want you to do, God helping you: Take your everyday, ordinary life—your sleeping, eating, going-to-work, and walking-around life—and place it before God as an offering. Embracing what God does for you is the best thing you can do for Him. Don't become so well-adjusted to your culture that you fit into it without even thinking. Instead, fix your attention on God. You'll be changed from the inside out. Readily recognize what He wants from you, and quickly respond to it. Unlike the culture around you, always dragging you down to its level of immaturity, God brings the best out of you, develops well-formed maturity in you* (Romans 12:1-2).

May this be a tool you can use to clear the ground of every obstruction and build a life of obedience into full maturity— the fully complete you!

Let the journey begin!

Being authentic is the ability to make self-honoring choices and stand firmly in who we are in our core. Being true to ourselves gives us the insight and com- passion to see others for who they are, not who we expect them to be. It frees us up from the judgment of ourselves and others and it gives others the free- dom to be themselves as well. —Victoria J. Reynolds

✳ ✳ *Search me, God, and know my heart; test me and know my anxious thoughts. See if there is any offensive way in me, and lead me in the way everlasting* (Psalm 139:23-24 NIV).

47

Chapter Five

The Journey

Until you make the unconscious conscious, it will direct your life and you will call it fate. —Carl Jung

It amazes me how little we are willing to invest in the most important asset we have—the one asset that governs everything else we experience in this life—our soul.

Many don't realize that when a soul feeds on toxic thoughts and falsehoods, just like when a body feeds on toxins in the form of imitation food substances, it slows down and ceases to operate at maximum capacity. That's when you need to commit to doing a deep cleanse and detoxifying not only your body, but also your soul. You need to abstain from the thoughts, habits, and behavioral patterns that undermine your destiny, purpose, and happiness. What are the mental barriers and roadblocks keeping you from living more authentically? What is undermining your courage and creativity? What is keeping you from fulfilling your greatest potential?

We are on a 40-day journey to not only fast from the things that erode and destroy your soul, but also to feast on the things that edify and nourish it. During the next 40 days, and hopefully everyday for the rest of your life, you will make it a priority to set aside time to fortify your inner life.

TAKE TIME TO TAKE CARE OF YOUR SOUL!

Fasting is not just about getting a handle on what you're eating, but what's eating at you—it's not just about abstaining from food, but from negative attitudes, thoughts, habits, and behaviors that keep you from maintaining a healthy relationship with God, with yourself, and with the world at large.

That relationship will require commitment—just like any quality relationship. Commitment to overcoming obstacles, setbacks, discomfort, inconvenience, uncertainty, or whatever it is that commonly erodes a healthy, vibrant relationship. Cultivating commitment over the next 40 days will be one of the most valuable outcomes you will achieve. Your strength of commitment is both a necessary ingredient as well as a life-transforming byproduct that will empower you to literally change your world.

If you commit to fully engaging in this process on a daily basis—fully completing the soul fast challenge—you will come to the end having spent the best 40 days of your life. You will find yourself living in a level of abundance you didn't imagine possible before.

The 40-Day Soul Fast takes place over eight weeks. Each week is divided into five days for the purpose of this guided journey. A 40-day fast commonly practiced in the Christian tradition, known as Lent, is followed six days a week and does not include Sundays. It begins on a Wednesday, known as Ash Wednesday, so that the first week is comprised of only four days. For simplicity's sake, however, I have taken our eight weeks and divided them evenly so that you can establish a regular routine Monday through Friday, allowing for weekends off so you can focus on family and worship or make up a missed day if necessary.

We will begin our 40-day journey by talking about capacity building. Week one of our eight-week venture focuses on "The Power of 40: Enlarging Your Capacity." This topic, as with each week's topic, is divided into five segments. The first day of each week provides an introduction to the other four days, with each day highlighting a different aspect of that week's focus. In week two, we will talk about "The Purpose of a Soul Fast: The Self-Leadership Challenge." In week three, we will discuss "The Nature of the Soul: The Essence of You." In week four, we address "The Properties of Thought: You Are What You Think." Week five brings us to "The Importance of Identity: Becoming a Master by Mastering Your Mind." In week six we look at "The Power of Words: Healing the Hole in Your Soul." In week seven, we begin wrapping up by dealing with "The Power of Doing: God's Chosen Fast." And in week eight, we conclude by "Sealing the Healing: The Cleansing Power of Love."

After each day's brief discussion of a topic related to that week's theme, you will conclude the day with a brief meditation on one of the 40 characteristics of an authentic person. This is where your journaling exercises are presented. They are bullet-pointed questions for you to ponder—and for lack of space here—to answer in a separate journal. *The 40 Day Soul Fast Journal* is also available, providing you with space to write your answers and reflections.

Between each day's topic focus and each day's characteristic is a quote that looks something like this:

> Only one who devotes himself to a cause with his whole strength and soul can be a true master. For this reason mastery demands all of a person. —Albert Einstein

After this break point, you will read a meditation about one of the 40 characteristics of an authentic person. This is where the question and prompts portion of each day is included. These "points to ponder" will look something like what you see below. As you work your way through each of the next 40 days, I want you to keep the following instructions and insights in mind about fasting:

- As Jesus taught His disciples, *"When you practice some appetite-denying discipline to better concentrate on God, don't make a production out of it. It might turn you into a small-time celebrity but it won't make you a saint. If you 'go into training' inwardly, act normal outwardly"* (Matt. 6:16).

- Christians are not the only ones who see the value in fasting. Other religions concur about the importance of fasting being an "inward practice." As we see from this quote taken from the Koran, "To fast is better for you, if only you knew it" (2:18), fasting is best practiced in the privacy of your own soul.

- Mahatma (which means "Great Soul") Gandhi, a proclaimed Buddhist and avid faster, stated, "What the eyes are for the outer world, fasts are for the inner." He added, "Fasting will bring spiritual rebirth to those of you who cleanse and purify your bodies. The light of the world will illuminate within you when you fast and purify yourself."

Give yourself adequate time and space to focus on nurturing your inner self. Part of the soul fast discipline is not allowing everyday distractions to deter you from cultivating the inner life of your soul. According to Andrew Murray, many people "are unable to stand against the temptations of the world, or of their old nature. They strive to do their best to fight against sin, and to serve God, but they have no strength. They have never really grasped the secret: The Lord Jesus will, every day from heaven continue His work in me. But on one condition—the soul must give Him time each day to impart His love and his grace. Time alone with the Lord Jesus each day is the indispensable condition of growth and power." Murray counsels: "Shut the world out, withdraw from all worldly thoughts and occupations, and shut yourself in alone with God, to pray to Him in secret. Let this be your chief object in prayer, to realize the presence of your heavenly Father." It will require disciplined focus, a heightened mindfulness, and keen sensitivity to the Spirit of God. I think of tennis legend Lindsay Davenport who was said to be "trespassing on her own purpose" as she played against Elena Likhovtseva in the 2001 US Open. Don't be caught trespassing on your own purpose by not paying attention to the process. God has already determined to make you a winner in life. The decision to cooperate with His will and to develop the champion within by cultivating your inner life depends entirely on you. You alone have the power to sabotage your victory.

As you enter into this 40-day journey, settle your spirit. Calm your mind. James Allen said, "Calmness of mind is one of the beautiful jewels of wisdom." Press into the presence of God—stay connected to that crucial lifeline. This will be critical to your success throughout the next eight weeks. As Mother Theresa so aptly observed: "The biggest problem facing the world today is not people dying in the streets of Calcutta, and not inflation, but spiritual deprivation—the feeling of emptiness associated with feeling separate from God, and from all our sisters and brothers on planet Earth." Stay connected to the Spirit and to the community around you—this is key to practicing authentic living.

When we are able to live authentically, we will be able to connect on a deeper level with all of humanity. We will become an unstoppable force as we collectively move toward a higher and greater good. Don't draw back, but press with me into this move toward unity. This is the heart of God for His people—to be of one mind and one spirit. This is where God commands His blessing (see Ps. 133). Authenticity requires a degree of connectivity—of genuine community and collaboration. Where there is separation, disconnection, and isolation, you will find confusion and deception. These timeless words from the Pulitzer Prize winning author Eudora Welty resonate with the longings of my own heart: "My continuing passion is to part a curtain, that invisible shadow that falls between people, the veil of indifference to each other's presence, each other's wonder, each other's human plight." This is true compassion and the central theme of the Gospel (see Matt. 25:34-40). *helpfulness, visit the sick, show kindness & compassion, feed hungry, show hospitality, visit those in prison. be kind to the poor.*

As we move out together, as a body, *"joined and knit together by what every joint supplies, according to the effective working by which every part does its share"* (Eph. 4:16 NKJV), may we continue to cultivate and grow and edify ourselves in the love of Christ. We are each more important than any one of us can know. We wield more power to change the course of history than any of us can imagine. All of us are always only one decision away from fulfilling our best destiny—and the world's best hope for peace.

Let's get started discovering the authentic you!

Living authentically is a journey of remembrance, acknowledging that we are powerful spiritual beings...to remember this truth; we need to move away from our mind's incessant chatter, and move directly into our hearts. This is the quiet space of our true essence, our knowing. Aligning our heart with the heart of God allows us to be in touch with our spirit. Each day we can request to see ourselves as God sees us, in all of our perfection, without judgment or expectations. We are no ordinary beings. We are powerful spirits destined to remember our greatness, our divine connection. It is time to remove the blocks. It is time to remember. —Kay Nuyens[1]

What good would it do to get everything you want and lose you, the real you? What could you ever trade your soul for? (Mark 8:36)

SECTION II

THE 40 DAY SOUL FAST

Week One

The Power of Forty: Enlarging Your Capacity

Day One

Transforming

It may be hard for an egg to turn into a bird: it would be a jolly sight harder for it to learn to fly while remaining an egg. We are like eggs at present. And you cannot go on indefinitely being just an ordinary, decent egg. We must be hatched or go bad. —C.S. Lewis

True self! Transformed life! Authentically me! Full potential! Who wouldn't want each of these? But as C.S. Lewis so duly noted, you can't learn to fly by remaining an egg. That's what this 40-day journey is all about—helping you break out of your shell, spread your wings, and jump free from the confines of your nest. After all, if you don't hatch, sooner or later, life will start to feel pretty rotten.

Transformation is a miraculous process. We see it taking place all throughout nature. For some of us, it is how we know God is at work on the earth. Every time a seed planted gives forth a harvest, or a great oak emerges from a tiny acorn, or a tulip breaks free from a bulb, we see the miracle of creation at work. Wherever growth and transformation are not taking place, there is stagnation and death.

Life involves movement and change. Where there is energy, there is vibration. Light and sound—everything you see and hear—is comprised of waves of vibrating particles, constantly moving. The atmosphere around you is actually alive with motion. All of reality—or what you perceive as

61

reality—is in constant flux. Your words, thoughts, and decisions impact the atmosphere, just as much as the atmosphere around you impacts what you think and say. There is a constant transaction—an interchange and exchange—of energy taking place at every level, from the solar activity that surrounds the earth to the subatomic particles that make up every living cell. Every breath you take, every bite you eat, every word you speak involves an energy exchange that results in transformation. You and I are simply walking, breathing transformers—energy conductors converting energy from one form into another. This is how energy is generated and ultimately how the process of creation takes place.

So it is when you exchange your old life for a new life in Christ. You become a new creation.

> *Therefore if any person is [ingrafted] in Christ (the Messiah) he is a new creation (a new creature altogether); the old [previous moral and spiritual condition] has passed away. Behold, the fresh and new has come* (2 Corinthians 5:17 AMP).

And so the transformation begins. As soon as you are "born again"[1] by the Spirit of God, a new life begins—a new journey of discovering and becoming your truest, most authentic self. Your *divine* self, created in God's image, infused with His very nature (see 2 Pet. 1:4). You have been seeded with the life of Christ by God's own Spirit, and as that life germinates within you, you become less of your former self and more of your divine, authentic self—you begin the metamorphosis of being changed from one degree of glory to another. As Paul wrote, you *"are being transformed into the same image from glory to glory, just as by the Spirit of the Lord"* (2 Cor. 3:18 NKJV). *The*

Message says it like this: *"Our lives gradually becoming brighter and more beautiful as God enters our lives and we become like Him."*

FULL EXPRESSION

The word *glory* connotes "the full expression of the potential of an object or person." The glory of the sun is its heat and light. The glory of a flower is its fragrance and beauty. The glory of a human being is fully expressing our God-like nature, for, according to Saint Irenaeus, an early church father, "the glory of God is man fully alive"—which is exactly how you are being transformed, one step at a time, into the real, God-glorifying, you. Theologian NT Wright puts it this way:

> As a believer, you are a shadow of your future self. There is a real you that is more you than you can even imagine; uniquely you that reflects Him. As you are indwelt by the Spirit, you do that more and more.[2]

From the time God started designing His creation, the number 40 has represented that transformational passage. Even the not-so-glamorous caterpillar realizes he is intended for greater things. So he sheds his old life, struggles to a higher place, attaches himself to a leaf, and risks everything to spin a cocoon and wait. He has done his part; now he waits for the Creator of the universe to do His. Forty days later, it is time for the no-longer-a-caterpillar to experience his breakthrough, the promise of living to his full potential—a caterpillar's true self—the magnificent, winged butterfly.

Sounds like such a safe and easy process to most people. But don't miss the words "risk," "his part," and "wait." Jesus told us in Matthew 6:15, *"If you refuse to do your part, you cut yourself off from God's part."* Reverend Larry Gerber, Pastor of Shepherd of the Hills Church in Sun City, Arizona, gives us a reality check regarding what it means to *risk* and *wait* by describing the difficult but miraculous transition as follows:

> A cocoon is where a caterpillar risks it all—where it enters total chaos, where it undergoes total rebuilding, where it dies to one way of locomotion and life and is born to a new way of living. A cocoon is where a caterpillar allows itself to disintegrate into a blob of gelatinous liquid without structure or identity so that it can emerge with sharpened sensory perceptions and breathtaking beauty.[3]

Interestingly, in biblical numerology, the number 40 relates to the period of probation before the fulfillment of a promise. It is the product of the factors *four* and *ten,* which represent "completion" and "divine order," respectively. It seems fitting that 40 is also the gestation period for a human. In 40 short weeks a microscopic seed planted in the womb transforms into a baby full of world-changing potential. But this new being must first let go of the safety of the womb by pushing through the confinement and darkness until at last emerging into the open and light. Like most humans being taken from their place of comfort, the infant does it kicking and screaming. Unlike the caterpillar, however, the destiny of each newborn child is known only to the Creator who shapes each uniquely by His Spirit, not only before birth but afterwards as well. The apostle John says:

> *When you look at a baby, it's just that: a body you can look at and touch. But the person who takes shape within is formed by something you can't see and touch—the Spirit— and becomes a living spirit* (John 3:6).

Giants of the faith like Noah, Moses, Elijah, and Jesus experienced God's transforming power of 40. Each was sustained for 40 days and then rewarded with supernatural manifestations of God. Noah was protected in the ark for 40 days while God cleansed the earth and then a covenant rainbow appeared. Moses fasted for 40 days and then God gave him the Ten Commandments. Elijah was miraculously sustained for 40 days before running for 40 more days with supernatural strength to Mount Horeb, where God appeared to him. Jesus fasted in the desert for 40 days and nights; then, after resisting the enemy's temptations, He was visited by angels who supernaturally provided for His needs. He left that place of sacrifice and went out in the power of the Holy Spirit to heal the sick, feed the hungry, and raise the dead.

Submitting to the power of 40 is about cleansing, aligning, preparing, and loosing—four powerful concepts we will discuss throughout the remainder of the week.

> This above all: to thine own self be true, and it must follow, as the night the day, thou canst not then be false to any man. —Shakespeare

Today, the first day of your journey to a more authentic life, begins with a focus on *awareness*. This is the first of 40 characteristics I have identified of someone who is living authentically—for how can you be truly yourself if you're not aware of who you truly are?

CHARACTERISTIC 1: AWARENESS

The soul is the seat of human reflective consciousness, passion, intelligence and acumen; housing the mind will and emotions. When God created the soul of humanity, our very soul gave us the awareness of self. We gained the ability to know ourselves not only as individuals, separate and apart from all other created entities, but also as social, compassionate, and spiritual beings with desires and emotions driven by a higher consciousness. We were given the ability to refer to the essence, character, and personality of our souls as "myself" and others as "her-self" or "him-self." Your soul gives you the ability of knowing, sensing, and responding.

The first step to living authentically is to be aware of who you are – the wonderful, intelligent, creative person God has made you; to grasp the fact that you are more than a body responding to your environment through your five physical senses. The second step is to be aware of the impact your thoughts, words, attitude, and behavior have upon others, the quality of your life, as well as the world in which you live—you are not an island. The third and final thing that you must be aware of is the unrealized potential for greatness that lies within you.

For now, I want you to simply focus on being more self-aware. Without cultivating self-awareness, nothing else you do will move you toward living more authentically. It is the first step you must take in making the adjustments necessary to correct the course of your life.

A.W. Tozer said, "Being has ceased to have much appeal for people, and doing engages almost everyone's attention. Modern Christians lack symmetry. They know almost nothing about the inner life." When you think about who you are, what does your internal dialogue tell you?

If you are to grow as a person, you must be aware of your internal dialogue—what your thoughts are telling you about who you are now and who you are capable of becoming. You must have an objective understanding of your own mindsets, habits, challenges, strengths, and weaknesses.

- Describe what you believe are some outstanding characteristics about yourself?

- How have you capitalized on those and harnessed the inherent power of you?

- What more can you do to maximize your unique set of gifts and minimize your own peculiar shortcomings?

Stop now to reflect and take responsibility for knowing yourself more completely. It was Socrates who so profoundly, yet simply, instructed, "Know thyself," and it was Shakespeare who, inspired by Socrates, wrote, "To thine own self be true!"

Embrace your personal responsibility to discover your purpose, mission, and assignment in life. As Paul advised the Corinthians, *"Examine your motives, test your heart"* (1 Cor. 11:27).

As you set out on this journey toward discovering your divine, authentic self—uncovering those things that truly motivate and inspire you and bring you inexplicable peace and joy, casting aside those things which chastise your peace and grieve your spirit—I want you to prayerfully lean into the Spirit of God within yourself. Listen carefully to what you hear God's Spirit saying—that still, small voice—and write down what you hear.

Use *The 40 Day Soul Fast Journal*, and answer the following 24 questions. (If you have not purchased one yet, find a notebook and designate it specifically to this 40-day adventure). If you don't know the answers, simply write down the questions and come back to them later. It is my prayer that by the end of the next 40 days, you will have a clearer understanding regarding the significance of who you truly are and why you are here at this particular point in history.

Ask yourself these 24 questions:

1. Who am I outside of the roles I play?

2. What are my long-term goals?

3. What should I be doing with my life right now?

4. What are my strengths?

5. What are my weaknesses?

6. What direction will my life go if I continue doing what I'm doing?

7. How can I be sure I am in the right place, doing the right thing?

8. What is my purpose?

9. Who should I be partnering with?

10. What resources are available for me to accomplish my goals?

11. Do I like the person I've become?

12. What do I really want to achieve in this lifetime?

13. What brings me my greatest joy?

14. What am I really passionate about?

15. What frustrates me most or makes me sad?

16. If I could do something other than what I am doing now, what would that be?

17. If I could live somewhere else, where would that be?

18. Do these things that I do and am involved with make me feel good and happy?

19. Are my relationships mutually beneficial and symbiotic?

20. Is there room for improvement in my relationships?

21. What have I accomplished so far with my life? Is it enough?

22. If I could do one thing different, what would it be?

23. After my death, will future generations know that I lived?

24. How do I want people to remember me?

When these questions keep you awake at night and make you listless during the day, set aside time to pray and journal your thoughts until you find the answers.

> We shall not cease from exploration
> And the end of all our exploring
> Will be to arrive where we started
> And know the place for the first time. —T. S. Eliot

God's Spirit touches our spirits and confirms who we really are (Romans 8:15).

Day Two

Cleansing

All religions exhort man to cleanse the heart of malice, greed, hate, and anger. All religions hold out the gift of Grace as the prize for success in this cleaning process. —Sri Sathya Sai Baba

Forty is a number of cleansing. In the time of Noah, God sent the rain for 40 days and nights in order to destroy that which was against His purposes. Gaining a greater capacity to acquire new wisdom, capitalize on opportunities, and maximize your potential requires getting rid of those things that are weighing you down and distracting you from your life's purpose. You need to get clear of whatever is obstructing your pathway to fulfilling your best destiny. This segment will help you eliminate the soul-killing clutter that is holding you back and keeping you from living a more abundant and authentic life.

If the stream of living water is going to flow unencumbered from the Source to you (see John 7:38), and then through you to the needy world around you, every hindrance to that flow must be eliminated. Any detours must be closed off that are preventing you from being clearly led of the Spirit. God's blessing on your life, your business, and your relationships begins with cleansing. In other words, clearing the airways in order to hear His voice more distinctly.

In Isaiah 58, God is very clear about wanting more than the self-deprivation exhibited by a sad face and the

71

wearing of sackcloth and ashes. Here He gives you His list of purpose-busters that He wants you—and everyone else—to be free of:

> *Is it a fast that I have chosen, a day for a man to afflict his soul? Is it to bow down his head like a bulrush, and to spread out sackcloth and ashes? Would you call this a fast, and an acceptable day to the Lord? Is this not the fast that I have chosen: To loose the bonds of wickedness, to undo the heavy burdens, to let the oppressed go free, and that you break every yoke?* (Isaiah 58:5-6 KJV)

Although the "bonds of wickedness" God is speaking of here refers to wrongdoing and sin, the definition also means more than simply breaking a set of rules. Think of sin as anything that keeps you from growing in Christ— keeps you from being transformed and changed from glory to glory—or anything that diminishes your true self. What are the things that cause you to stagnate or live in accordance with your former self that was *"dead in trespasses and sins"*—that cause you to live *"in the past [when] you were dead because you sinned and fought against God"* (Eph. 2:1 CEV). Remember, wherever there is stagnation, there is death.

God knows your heart; He created it. And He knows what will bring life to it.

> *Investigate my life, O God, find out everything about me; cross-examine and test me, get a clear picture of what I'm about; see for Yourself whether I've done anything wrong—then guide me on the road to eternal life* (Psalm 139:23-24).

A PATH TO FREEDOM

When Isaiah spoke of undoing heavy burdens, he was talking about those things that dictate the direction your life moves in. The word suggests a yoke that was placed on a younger ox attaching it to an older ox, and thus the older ox determined the younger's direction. Your negative thoughts can act like that yoke, making you believe that who you once were, where you have come from, or what people have said about you are the determining factors of your destiny. Nothing could be further from the truth. God wants to set you free from that kind of thinking during this 40-day fast.

When Isaiah spoke of letting the oppressed go free, he was talking about creating an environment of liberty—an atmosphere free from condemnation. Oppression is a reference to the crushing weight of powerlessness, guilt, and shame that can hold you down. Break free from self-condemnation. Whatever shame is causing you to cower and be bowed under—to think less of yourself than you should—is a lie being whispered in your ear by the enemy of your soul. Jesus took care of it at the Cross. *"There is therefore now no condemnation to them which are in Christ"* (Rom. 8:1 KJV).

Sometimes we are our own worst enemy. Are you sabotaging your own success by the thoughts you think? Are you allowing those thoughts to interfere with how you manage your time? Or are you giving someone else permission to lay things on you that aren't yours to carry and don't further you toward your destiny? Are your past failures holding dominion over your future? Are relationships distracting you, or worse, crushing the life right out of you? By identifying those things that only you—with the help of the Holy Spirit—can pinpoint, you can begin to eliminate from your soul the toxins that keep you bound in negativity, unrest, confusion, fear, and despair.

Free yourself from heavy burdens! Break free from oppression! Cleanse your mind of the thoughts that weigh you down. Replace your toxic thoughts and polluted mindset with the light of the truth from the Word of God about who you really are in Christ—put on *"the mind of Christ"* (1 Cor. 2:16 NKJV), for *"whoever...[having the mind of Christ] is done with [intentional] sin [has stopped pleasing himself and the world, and pleases God]"* (1 Pet. 4:1 AMP). Pray as David did: *"May all my thoughts be pleasing to Him"* (Ps. 104:34 NLT).

> Our life is what our thoughts make it. —Marcus Aurelius Antoninus

As we move through day two of our 40-day soul fast, I want to talk to you about the second characteristic of an authentic person: *Godliness.* Godliness begins with the "God-likeness" of your thoughts—the thoughts that govern your mind. It begins by putting on the mind of Christ.

CHARACTERISTIC 2: GODLINESS

Fasting or abstinence is not an end in itself, but rather a door that is opened to us for the purpose of godly living. To me, godliness is synonymous to Christ-likeness. At the dawn of the nineteenth century, the Scottish Professor, A.J. Gossip said:

> You will not stroll into Christ-likeness with your hands in your pockets, shoving the door open with a careless shoulder. This is no hobby for one's leisure moments, taken up at intervals when we have nothing much to

do, and put down and forgotten when our life grows full and interesting. It takes all one's strength, and all one's heart, and all one's mind, and all one's soul, given freely and recklessly and without restraint.

A gospel that is preached that makes no mention of godliness is not the true Gospel: "True godliness leaves the world convinced beyond a shadow of a doubt that the only explanation for you, is Jesus Christ to whose eternally unchanging and altogether adequate 'I AM!' your heart has learned to say with unshatterable faith, 'Thou art!'" said the great theologian, Major Ian Thomas.

Paul touches on the concept of godliness no less than nine times in his first letter to Timothy. He instructs Timothy to *"exercise yourself toward godliness,"* and that *"godliness is profitable for all things,"* adding that *"godliness with contentment is great gain"* (1 Tim. 4:7,8; 6:6 NKJV). There is a kind of gospel being proclaimed today which conveniently accommodates itself to the spirit of the age and makes no demand for godliness.

Peter emphasized this characteristic as well. He wrote, *"By His divine power, God has given us everything we need for living a godly life"* (2 Pet. 1:3 NLT). Then he spelled it out more plainly by detailing the seven things we must add to our faith in order to "abound and be fruitful" or *"more productive and useful"* (2 Pet. 1:8 NLT).

> *Supplement your faith with a generous provision of moral excellence, and moral excellence with knowledge, and knowledge with self-control, and self-control with patient endurance, and patient endurance with godliness, and godliness with brotherly affection, and brotherly affection with love for everyone* (2 Peter 1:5-7 NLT).

It is godliness that provides the bridge between "patience" and "kindness"—it is what causes our virtue and knowledge and temperance to translate into the most God-like characteristic of all: *love*—for "*God is love*" (1 John 4:8).

I encourage you today to do a thorough study of the word *godliness* and meditate on all it implies. Then ask yourself where you are falling short of it. Eliminate those things that are not "adding to your faith" and supplement those key things Peter listed that will "*have your life on a firm footing*" (2 Pet. 1:10)!

This is ultimately the purpose of *The 40 Day Soul Fast!* To run a diagnostic on the life of your soul and purge whatever is keeping you from being more productive and useful. As Paul wrote to Titus:

> *We're being shown how to turn our backs on a godless, indulgent life, and how to take on a God-filled, God-honoring life. This new life is starting right now, and is whetting our appetites for the glorious day when our great God and Savior, Jesus Christ, appears. He offered Himself as a sacrifice to free us from a dark, rebellious life into this good, pure life, making us a people He can be proud of, energetic in goodness* (Titus 2:12-14).

- In what areas are you living "*a godless, indulgent life*" and how can you—starting right now—begin living a more "*God-filled, God-honoring life?*"

As Paul wrote the Corinthians, "*Examine your motives, test your heart!*" (1 Cor. 11:27). Make sure everything you say, do, think, and choose is lined up with who it is you truly want to be. Check your heart. Clean house by sweeping up any impure motives or stray intentions. Pay attention to how the things you harbor within your heart affect your words and behaviors—and equally important, how your words, habits, and behaviors affect the life of your soul.

It is my own firm belief that the strength of the soul grows in proportion as you subdue the flesh. — Mohandas Gandhi

Since Jesus went through everything you're going through and more, learn to think like Him. Think of your sufferings as a weaning from that old sinful habit of always expecting to get your own way. Then you'll be able to live out your days free to pursue what God wants instead of being tyrannized by what you want (1 Peter 4:1).

Day Three

Aligning

Just as your car runs more smoothly and requires less energy to go faster and farther when the wheels are in perfect alignment, you perform better when your thoughts, feelings, emotions, goals, and values are in balance. —Brian Tracy

The number 40 is associated with repentance and realignment. God through Jonah gave the Ninevites 40 days to repent. The word *repentance* is often linked with sin, but the word is actually a life-giving word that refers to turning and going another, better way. It refers to changing how you think and process information. God wants to give you a new context for living. He wants to change the pattern of your thinking by realigning your thought life. If your thinking is straight your life will be straight. How can you realign your life so that it reflects the authentic you God had in mind? You can meditate on the Word of God (see Josh. 1:8). Through study of the Word of God you renew your mind (see Rom. 12:1-2). When your mind is renewed, true life in Christ Jesus is restored. What a promise we find in John when Jesus declared, *"I am the Bread of Life. The person who aligns with me hungers no more and thirsts no more, ever"* (John 6:35).

Coming into alignment with Christ is the only way to discover your true self. Letting someone else lead and giving up control may be a new adventure for you—but He promises the process is worthwhile.

Anyone who intends to come with Me has to let Me lead. You're not in the driver's seat; I am. Don't run from suffering; embrace it. Follow Me and I'll show you how. Self-help is no help at all. Self-sacrifice is the way, My way, to saving yourself, your true self. What good would it do to get everything you want and lose you, the real you? What could you ever trade your soul for? (Mark 8:34)

SAVING YOUR TRUE SELF

How do you keep from losing the real you in a world of distractions? The cultural forces pulling you to do or have more can cause you to lose sight of how to simply *be*. Learning to listen to your own voice, let alone the "still, small voice of God," in the din and hubbub of life's deafening cares and concerns can be an enormous challenge. Sometimes you just need to pull away, disconnect, or as Solomon told his beloved, *"Rise up, my love, my fair one, and come away"* (Song of Sol. 2:10 NKJV).

Throughout the Bible, God caused His people to "come away." He compelled prophets and patriarchs to pull away from society in order to learn how to listen to their heart and be led of His Spirit. Every great leader God raised up had a 40-day, or more often, a 40-year, "alignment period"—from Moses to David to Jesus. Undoubtedly Moses came under the power of 40 more than any other person in the Bible. After 40 years in Pharaoh's house, Moses judged wrongly how to right what he saw happening in his sphere of influence. God then led him to the desert for 40 more years of paradigm shifting. After God empowered Moses to lead the Israelites out of Egypt, he spent 40 additional years trying to change the mindset of a nation.

Forty can also be seen as ten times four. Where ten is the number of law, and four is the number of the Earth, we see God bringing the things of the Earth back into divine alignment with His law. That's what Jesus meant when He taught us to pray, *"Your kingdom come. Your will be done on earth as it is in heaven"* (Matt. 6:10 NKJV). These commands and principles are intended to give you forwarding power to become your true self—to cause the real you to come into alignment.

Your physical body is the holder of your potential and is the means used to advance you in God's Kingdom. Try going somewhere without it! Do you need to change the way you treat it, bringing your physical and emotional health into alignment with God's ways? Do you need to be more intentional about practicing the Sabbath so you can enter into God's rest (see Heb. 4:6,10 NKJV) where *"you will find rest for your souls"* (Jer. 6:16; Matt. 11:29 NKJV)? Or do you simply need go to bed earlier so you get the physical rest you need? This is God's will concerning you! Your refreshment and rest is a priority to Him. He said, *"I'll refresh tired bodies; I'll restore tired souls"* (Jer. 31:25).

What about other areas that can get out of alignment and cause unrest? For example, are you operating your business according to God's principles? Are your marriage and other relationships lived according to His ways? Do you handle your finances in a way that allows God to bless you with more? If not, during this 40-day fast, repent and go a different way.

Be careless in your dress if you will, but keep a tidy soul. —Mark Twain

As we progress on our journey toward authenticity, we have talked about being more self-aware and about the importance of pursuing godliness. To help us do both more fully, we must be willing to take an honest look at our lives and be willing to seek the truth about who we are now versus who God calls us to be in Christ.

CHARACTERISTIC 3: TRUTH

Yesterday we explored the characteristic of godliness—or God-likeness—concluding that if "God is love," then loving like God is one way to practice being godlier. Yet the first thing Jesus told His disciples to do after He completed His earthly ministry was to wait on the Spirit of Truth, which He would send to help and empower them.

> *He'll provide you another Friend so that you will always have someone with you. This Friend is the Spirit of Truth. The godless world can't take Him in because it doesn't have eyes to see Him, doesn't know what to look for* (John 14:15).

Love and truth go hand in hand. "*Your love and truth are all that keeps me together*" (Ps. 40:11). "*Guilt is banished through love and truth*" (Prov. 16:6), and "*Love and truth form a good leader; sound leadership is founded on loving integrity*" (Prov. 20:28).

The foundational key to living authentically is truth. Not only being true to yourself, but living in the full light of the truth and being governed by the Spirit of Truth.

> *When the Spirit of truth comes, He will guide you into all truth. He will not speak on His own but will tell you what*

He has heard. He will tell you about the future (John 16:13 NLT).

- Sit quietly with that Spirit today.

- Invite the Holy Spirit to guide you into the truth about yourself—*all* the truth.

- Ask Him to help you filter through what is not of the truth, to cut anything away from your heart or mind that is not true, and to help you cultivate those things that lead *"to finding yourself, your true self"* (Luke 9:23).

As the psalmist wrote, *"What You're after is truth from the inside out. Enter me, then; conceive a new, true life"* (Ps. 51:6).

- What would this new, true life look like if it were conceived in you?

Remember, anyone daring to live authentically must first and foremost be honest with themselves and others. The worst of all deceptions is self-deception. Truth liberates the soul from self-deception. Always speak the truth. Exemplify truth. Uphold the truth. Stand on the truth. *Live the truth!*

Leaders of the future will have the courage to align with principles and go against the grain of old assumptions or paradigms. It takes tremendous courage and stamina to say, "I'm going to align my personal value system, my lifestyle, my direction, and my habits with timeless principles." —Stephen Covey

You with open minds; truth-ready minds will see it at once. Prefer my life-disciplines over chasing after money, and God-knowledge over a lucrative career. For Wisdom is better than all the trappings of wealth; nothing you could wish for holds a candle to her (Proverbs 8:9-11).

Day Four

Preparing

Spectacular achievement is always preceded by spectacular preparation. —Robert H. Schuller

In Matthew 4, Jesus was led by the Spirit into the desert where He fasted and prayed for 40 days and nights. It was a time of preparation for the opposition that would follow, but also for the opportunities ahead of Him. Paul understood that combination as well. He wrote in First Corinthians 16:9, *"A huge door of opportunity for good work has opened up here. (There is also mushrooming opposition.)"* Cleansing and aligning your soul prepares you spiritually, emotionally, and mentally to bring the seed of purpose planted in you to complete fruition and to deal with the enemy's plan to uproot it. But no small thinking!

Before God brought Adam on the scene, He had already prepared a life-giving place where he could not only live physically but also purposefully—the whole Earth! God is preparing you, but He is also preparing a place of purpose and abundance. He is getting ready to birth acts of faith through you; but again you must do your part:

> *Clear lots of ground for your tents! Make your tents large. Spread out! Think big! Use plenty of rope, drive the tent pegs deep. You're going to need lots of elbow room for your growing family. You're going to take over whole nations; you're going to resettle abandoned cities. Don't be afraid— you're not going to be embarrassed. Don't hold back—you're not going to come up short* (Isaiah 54:2-4).

Ask the Spirit to reveal to you those things that need to go so you have room for what's coming. Cooperate with Heaven's cultivation process. Do not settle for living a mediocre life characterized by limitations and restrictions. This *40 Day Soul Fast* should not be viewed as one that is restricting you, but preparing you for greatness, power, and uncommon success. Jesus embraced His time of preparation over a 40-day period too and passed His three tests in the desert by relying on Scripture and refusing to settle for anything less than His destiny. Rather than accept the glory offered by satan, Jesus purposed to bring His Father glory by completing the path laid out for Him. Spend time meditating on God's Word during these 40 days so that when the opposition comes you can rebuke the enemy and cause him to flee by speaking God's Word.

Opportunity and prosperity are enviable outcomes of this soul fast. Many people today believe that godliness is equivalent to poverty, but the Word says, *"Beloved, I pray that in all respects you may prosper and be in good health, just as your soul prospers"* (3 John 1:2 NKJV). When you are willing to use your gifts and talents to your full potential, God will provide the place that maximizes them. He is also going to supernaturally provide unexpected opportunities and wonderful surprises. When reading the parable of the talents in Matthew 25, most people focus on the servant who did not produce a return on the talent he was given. But did you notice that his talent was unexpectedly given to the one who had produced the most return on his investment? It was not an opportunity he had worked to produce, but one that was unexpectedly presented by the Master.

When the Israelites stood before the Promised Land and God was ready to give it to them, they were asked to first spy out the land, which they did for 40 days. They brought out branches of grapes so large they had to be supported on poles between two men. It was obvious the opportunities there were great, but they chose to focus on the opposition instead of the opportunity. Ask God to give you new eyes to see opportunities and the mental, spiritual, and emotional preparation to overcome opposition.

> Only a man who knows what it is like to be defeated can reach down to the bottom of his soul and come up with the extra ounce of power it takes to win.
> —Muhammad Ali

Preparation requires commitment. If you are reading this, you have already demonstrated this characteristic and are well on our way to living truer to your authentic self. Continue to cultivate commitment by sticking with this 40-day endeavor to the very end! It is this steadfast endurance that will strengthen and purify your soul like nothing else.

CHARACTERISTIC 4: COMMITMENT

Commitment liberates the mind. Commitment to your purpose, goals, or values will free your mind from cultural, political, and social entanglements so your soul is free to connect more deeply with one's true self and God.

Your flesh wants comfort and pleasure, but your soul and spirit desire growth and significance.

Your mind is always in contemplation of opposites and options: Should I eat home or dine out? Should I watch television or pray? Should I call in sick or get up and go to work? Should I stay up and finish my report or go to bed and finish it in the morning? We are all caught in a world of decisions, filled with fork-in-the-road experiences and options—critical moments in time when our values find their truest expression once that decision is made.

Commitment requires faith. You must not only have faith in God, but faith in the person who God has made you to be.

That faith will be tested along the way. The testing and try-ing of your faith, the refining of your intentions and resolve, the dedication, determination, and perseverance required to stick with something until you've obtained the desired outcome will empower and liberate you—and expand your capacity to do even more. Jesus told His disciples, *"By your steadfastness and patient endurance you shall win the true life of your souls"* (Luke 21:19 AMP).

- In light of "thinking bigger" as we discussed above, what would your life look like if you were to actually "win the true life of your soul?" Imagine it now.

You must be persistent and steadfast in pursuing that authentic, true life that God created you to experience in your present life here on the Earth. It's not a "done deal" when you receive Christ Jesus as your Lord. Paul wrote that you must *"work out your own salvation with fear and trembling"* (Phil. 2:12). The *Amplified Bible* breaks it down further:

> *...Work out (cultivate, carry out to the goal, and fully complete) your own salvation with reverence and awe and trembling (self-distrust, with serious caution, tenderness of conscience, watchfulness against temptation, timidly shrinking from whatever might offend God and discredit the name of Christ) (Philippians 2:12 AMP).*

You must continue to *"believe to the saving of the soul"* (Heb. 10:39 NKJV). It takes commitment. You must be committed to doing whatever is necessary to save your true self. Jesus said:

Self-sacrifice is the way, My way, to saving yourself, **your true self.** *What good would it do to get everything you want and lose you,* **the real you?** *What could you ever trade your soul for?* (Mark 8:37)

- What are you going to commit to doing in order to save the real you?

- Identify one thing you should purge from your life that is causing you to lose the real you.

- List one thing you should practice every day that will help cultivate your truest self.

If you plan to live an authentic life, and to both become and do all that God has created you to be and do, it will take commitment. This *40 Day Soul Fast* is designed to help you cultivate commitment so that you can cultivate your most true self. Don't cheat yourself out of experiencing life at its most abundant, prosperous level—stay committed to living authentically.

During this 40-day period you will encounter many obstacles and be tempted to abandon the daily disciplines. You may even reach the point of wanting to give up on believing in yourself or feel that there are other things preventing you from completing this wonderfully enriching and empowering experience.

Don't let small things keep you from your bigger self! I ask my audiences everywhere I go, "What is the one thing you can change that will change everything?" You will be surprised at what a difference one small adjustment can make in your life—a minor thing that can keep you from or move you toward major success. Sometimes it's just a matter of being consistent and staying with it—as Jesus told His disciples, *"Staying with it—that's what is required. Stay with it to the end. You won't be sorry"* (Luke 21:19).

Lack of commitment could be the only thing standing between you and what you really want.

A little more persistence, a little more effort, and what seemed hopeless failure may turn to glorious success. —Elbert Hubbard

Your heart's been in the right place all along. You've got what it takes to finish it up, so go to it. Once the commitment is clear, you do what you can, not what you can't. The heart regulates the hands (2 Corinthians 8:10).

Day Five

Loosing

Faith is taking the first step even when you don't
see the whole staircase. —Martin Luther King, Jr.

At the end of this *40 Day Soul Fast*, God is going to send a new you out into a new place. Not just the same old you with a few add-ons. That would be like hot-gluing a pair of wings on a caterpillar! For you to make the metamorphosis into a beautiful, winged butterfly capable of taking flight, you will have to develop extraordinary faith and patience. This is why cultivating the life of your soul is so very important—and why these are among the key strengths 40 carries the power to help you accomplish.

The number 40 can be expressed as five times eight; eight represents new beginnings and five is the number of grace. Forty empowers you with the grace you need to step out and take firm hold of your future. It will expand your capacity to see beyond your present limitations and to focus on the promise of future possibilities. Your divine self has a divine destiny orchestrated by God. He has called and anointed you to step forward, to *"be strong and courageous"* (Josh. 1:9 NIV) and take possession of all He has prepared for you. Paul told the Ephesians:

> *Awake, O sleeper, and arise from the dead, and Christ*
> *shall shine (make day dawn) upon you and give you light*
> (Ephesians 5:14 AMP).

In other words, you need to wake up and see the light about who God has called you to be in Christ. The greatness He has seeded in you with His own Spirit—the power you wield because of that Spirit working in and through you. Don't be like a walking dead person—wake up from the coma you're in and start living and impacting the world around you. It might not feel like it because you're not yet fully awake—perhaps you're still drowsy from disappointments and distractions—but you are destined for greatness.

Champions like Abraham, Joseph, Moses, Joshua, and David were all destiny-minded—they saw past their situations and limitations to what was possible with God's grace and anointing. You, too, must choose to focus on your potential in Christ rather than your position on Earth and march aggressively on toward the destiny God has called you to. Don't be like others who God anointed and blessed, but who refused to be loosed.

The Bible uses the word *loosed* throughout both the Old and New Testaments to indicate someone who has been set free from their former life and sent out, so to speak, to accomplish an ordained mission or goal. In the case of Ephraim, however, we read about a situation where there was a refusal to move out when the time came: *"When birth pangs signaled it was time to be born, Ephraim was too stupid to come out of the womb. When the passage into life opened up, he didn't show"* (Hos. 13:13). Instead, when the time is fulfilled and the due date comes, we need to pursue God's leading through prayer as David did and allow Him to lead us to a glorious destiny.

Noah, who endured the 40 days and nights of rain, was launched into a fresh new start with God's blessing and His command to lavish life on the Earth. At the end of Jesus' 40 days in the desert He was loosed to return to Galilee, where news spread quickly of His exploits.

> *From there He went all over Galilee. He used synagogues for meeting places and taught people the truth of God. God's kingdom was His theme—that beginning right now they were under God's government, a good government! He also healed people of their diseases and of the bad effects of their bad lives. Word got around the entire Roman province of Syria. People brought anybody with an ailment, whether mental, emotional, or physical. Jesus healed them, one and all* (Matthew 4:23-24).

God's blessing on your life can't be hidden; He sets you on a lamp stand to expel the darkness in this world where you were created, gifted, and anointed to make a difference. That's the amazing picture we see painted by the prophet Zechariah as he told of a time when other nations would see the blessing of God on His people:

> *The leaders will confer with one another: "Shouldn't we try to get in on this? Get in on God's blessings? Pray to God-of-the-Angel-Armies? What's keeping us? Let's go!" Lots of people, powerful nations—they'll come to Jerusalem looking for what they can get from God-of-the-Angel-Armies, looking to get a blessing from God. A Message from God-of-the-Angel-Armies: "At that time, ten men speaking a variety of languages will grab the sleeve of one Jew, hold tight, and say, 'Let us go with you. We've heard that God is with you'"* (Zechariah 8:21-23).

Don't draw back when destiny calls. Take firm hold of what God has called you to do in faith. Believe what God says about you, and determine in your heart to be among those whom people will grab onto saying, *"Let us go with you. We've heard that God is with you."*

> Ordinary riches can be stolen; real riches cannot. In your soul are infinitely precious things that cannot be taken from you. —Oscar Wilde

Yesterday we talked about commitment. Once you've committed to an endeavor, you will need patience to see it through to completion.

CHARACTERISTIC 5: PATIENCE

Patience will refine and perfect you. Patience is a discipline you must practice if you want to break free from the myriad of things that can plague and pollute your soul! Impatience will cause you all sorts of emotional and relational problems, such as losing your temper and saying things you will later regret; becoming agitated, anxious, stressed, frustrated, angry, flustered, and so on. Without patience, you won't be able to cultivate other important characteristics, such as self-control, compassion, faithfulness, mercy, and love. Impatience will cause you to get out of step with the Spirit of God, whose lead you are to closely follow.

I came across a compelling story that demonstrates the value and power of patience. This story is about a very unique plant, the Chinese bamboo. When bamboo is planted, watered, and nurtured throughout the growing season, it does not outwardly develop at all—not a bud or sprout appears. It takes five consecutive years of cultivation before even the slightest sign of growth is visible. And then in the fifth year, something incredible happens: Within a six-week period it grows up to 60 feet!

For five years, the bamboo seed silently develops underground—expanding its root system in order to make it strong enough to sustain the "sudden growth" that ultimately takes place in the fifth year. Had the tree failed to build a strong underground foundation, it would be impossible for it to "all of a sudden" reach its full potential when it comes time to push its way through the soil into the outside world.

This story illustrates the vital importance of patience in developing the character necessary to persevere and "push through." Like the bamboo, living true to your self and greatest potential takes patience and perseverance. People may not immediately see growth, but with the help of God, you will emerge as the great soul and admirable person your were created to be.

Henry Wadsworth Longfellow said, "The heights by great men, reached and kept, were not attained by sudden flight. But they, while their companions slept, toiled ever upward through the night."

Growth is a process and does not happen overnight. You must be steadfast and unshakeable in your faith. Former president of the Philippines Corazon Aquino said, "Faith is not simply a patience that passively suffers until the storm is past. Rather, it is a spirit that bears things - with resignations, yes, but above all, with blazing, serene hope."

Whatever you are believing God for, continue to trust, pray, and wait. Time is never wasted when you wait upon the Lord. As Paul wrote the Romans, *"We are enlarged in the waiting. We, of course, don't see what is enlarging us. But the longer we wait, the larger we become"* (Romans 8:25). And as James encouraged his readers, *"Let patience have its perfect work, that you may be perfect and complete, lacking nothing"* (James 1:4 NKJV).

Jesus said that it is only by exercising patience that you will learn to *"possess your soul"* (Luke 21:19 NKJV). As you draw closer to your authentic self, you must learn to take possession of your soul by mastering the discipline of patience. Stop, breathe, count to ten, do whatever you need to!

- What typically causes you to lose your patience?

- How can you change your perspective to tap into the power of patience?

- Visualize yourself exercising patient restraint the next time you want to react otherwise.

According to Galatians 5, patience is a fruit of the Spirit that you can cultivate simply by spending time in the presence of God—or rather, by letting the presence of God spend time in you, for it is *"the work which His presence within accomplishes!"* (Gal. 5:22 AMP). Developing patience is key to growing into your authentic self and fulfilling your best destiny: *"For you have need of steadfast patience and endurance, so that you may perform and fully accomplish the will of God"* (Heb. 10:36 AMP).

If one advances confidently in the direction of his dreams and endeavors to live the life which he has imagined, he will meet with a success unexpected in common hours. —Henry David Thoreau

We continue to shout our praise even when we're hemmed in with troubles, because we know how troubles can

develop passionate patience in us, and how that patience in turn forges the tempered steel of virtue, keeping us alert for whatever God will do next (Romans 5:3-4).

Week Two

The Purpose of a Soul Fast: The Self-Leadership Challenge

Day Six

Connecting

> The biggest problem facing the world today is not people dying in the streets of Calcutta, and not inflation, but spiritual deprivation...this feeling of emptiness associated with feeling separate from God, and from all our sisters and brothers on planet earth. —Mother Teresa

Emptiness. That's what most people think about when you discuss the subject of fasting. Mother Teresa had in mind the kind of emptiness that has little to do with food and everything to do with imitation fulfillments—experiences, events, habits, relationships, faulty desires and objectives, even spirits—that continually ensnare your soul, holding you back from moving confidently forward in the direction of your dreams. They can become a self-perpetuating process of defeat, failure, and despair and are killers of the creativity and innovation God wants to bring to the world through you. The purpose of fasting is to re-connect with God, allowing Him to set you free of those things that weigh you down, keeping you from running the race He has set before you and living your authentic life.

The good news is that you aren't stuck where you are now! You are on a journey with the Creator of the universe, and He doesn't intend for you to be trapped in your circumstances. It may take courage to risk facing the reality of where you are now, but knowledge of the truth will bring freedom. According to D.H. Lawrence, "The great virtue in life is real courage that knows how to face facts and live beyond them." Taking time to look within yourself and nurture your inner life will enable you to go beyond your former self.

Investing in you is worth it—spirit, soul, *and* body. Your body, the container of your potential, is the only vehicle your soul has to carry out your life on this Earth. When you fast with the intention of hearing God more clearly—either physically or strictly in relation to the life of your soul—the Holy Spirit will reveal the roadblocks, encourage repentance, and bring transformation.

Fasting is an ancient practice. Daniel, David, Elijah, and Esther fasted. The disciples of John the Baptist, the apostle Paul, and the early church members all had regular times of fasting. However, this powerful spiritual discipline has almost disappeared in Christian circles. Although people tend to think of fasting as denying one's self, it really is more about exchanging something of lesser value for something of greater value. It is exchanging the needs of the physical body for those of the spirit. The apostle Paul, who fasted regularly, saw that everything he gave up had little value compared to what he gained:

> *More than that, I count all things to be loss in view of the surpassing value of knowing Christ Jesus my Lord, for whom I have suffered the loss of all things, and count them but rubbish so that I may gain Christ* (Philippians 3:8 NASB).

T.S. Eliot once asked, "Where is the life we have lost in living?" Urgency and short cuts have become addictions. The thrill of being the hero, the last-minute wonderworker, comes with an enormous price tag. Eugene Peterson believes, "The faster we move the less we become; our very speed diminishes us."[1]

Fasting is about restraining your natural pleasures and breaking the cycle of stressful living by taking the time to seek God's face, the only One who sees your heart and knows who the authentic you really is. God has the power to break through the clutter that masks your identity, distracts your focus, and keeps you from the abundant life that Jesus died to provide.

You don't have to persuade God of your value or struggle to get Him to notice you. You are His beloved. Jesus said it this way in Matthew 6:32: *"What I'm trying to do here is to get you to relax, to not be so preoccupied with getting, so you can respond to God's giving."* Humble yourself before God, voluntarily submitting yourself to weakness, limitations, and to feasting on His Word; expect His grace to save your soul by healing, empowering, directing, and seeing.

> Prayer is not asking. It is a longing of the soul. It is daily admission of one's weakness. It is better in prayer to have a heart without words than words without a heart. —Mahatma Gandhi

Capacity building is what *The 40 Day Soul Fast* is all about. You are setting aside this time to enlarge, expand, and build your capacity to discover, create, become, and achieve more. As you put the first week of *The 40 Day Soul Fast* behind you, I commend you on your commitment to become more self-aware, to continue learning and discovering who God created you to be, the courage you have exhibited in uncovering and facing what may be hard truths, and the patience with which you are pursing it all.

The 40 Day Soul Fast is for the purpose of creating in you the capacity to hear and receive God's *best plan* for your life.

May you be among those, as Jesus said, *"to whom [the capacity to receive] it has been given"* (Matt. 19:11 AMP).

CHARACTERISTIC 6: CAPACITY

As you move forward on this journey to authenticity, know that the Spirit of God is working with you to increase your capacity to live more fully from your divine, authentic self. David wrote, "You have given me the capacity to hear and obey" (see Ps. 40:6). Take time to reflect on what you are hearing the Lord say this week. Press in and focus on discerning the Lord's voice amidst all the static and clutter around you. Clear the ground wherever you are by making room for the presence of God—let Him come and burn up the overgrowth and chaff in your life.

Above all, keep it simple. Learn from the words of King Solomon: *"Make the most of what God gives, both the bounty and the capacity to enjoy it, accepting what's given and delighting in the work"* (Eccles. 5:19).

- What have you learned about yourself so far?

- What are four things you will purpose to eliminate?

- What four new habits will you focus on cultivating?

Be open to receiving the gifts God is showing you and accessing everything God's Spirit is longing to do in your life. Increase your capacity to do and be more by increasing your capacity to walk in His Spirit and be led by His Spirit.

Spirit can be known only by spirit—God's Spirit and our spirits in open communion. Spiritually alive, we have access to everything God's Spirit is doing (1 Corinthians 2:14b).

Every day of this 40-day soul fast you should be growing more spiritually alive! You should be increasing your capacity to access everything God's Spirit is doing!

Where the spirit does not work with the hand there is no art. —Leonardo da Vinci

The unspiritual self, just as it is by nature, can't receive the gifts of God's Spirit. There's no capacity for them (1 Corinthians 2:14a).

Day Seven

Healing

*Pain insists upon being attended to. God whispers
to us in our pleasures, speaks in our consciences,
but shouts in our pains. It is His megaphone to
rouse a deaf world. —C.S. Lewis*

The Reverend Franklin Hall has been famously quoted as stating, "Fasting brings you into direct contact with unbelief so that it can be [healed and] removed." It isn't truth that controls you, but what you believe to be true. When Jesus healed the two blind men in Matthew 9:29, He asked them if they believed that He could heal them. When they said yes, He touched their eyes and said, "Become what you believe." What if Jesus made you the same offer today? What would you believe about what you can become?

Therapist and author Dr. Patrick Carnes tells the story of a hypnosis patient who was warned that the psychiatrist would place a hot coal in her hand while she was under hypnosis. As you might expect, when the doctor instead placed an ice cube in her hand, the patient responded as if it were a hot coal—she jerked her hand back. Beliefs are very powerful. But what you might not anticipate was that the woman's hand produced a blister![1] What you believe determines what you become.

Fasting allows the Holy Spirit to reshape you into your true self by dealing with your wounds from the past that have distorted, stagnated, and stunted your essence. Negative actions and reactions are often the outcry of a hurting soul.

You become the hurting that hurts and the disappointed that disappoints. Your soul becomes incarcerated in prisons of offense, resentment, and unforgiveness.

How you see yourself is based on what's been reflected back to you through events and words expressed by others. Those words and images govern and control your life, forcing you to develop coping skills in order to get through life with minimal pain and rejection. These negative patterns prevent you from fulfilling your dreams. They cause you to doubt yourself so that the seeds of potential die locked inside of you—all because your soul remains unhealed.

During this time of fasting, allow the Holy Spirit to show you people you need to forgive. Unforgiveness is like a leaking reservoir; water flows in, but drains out again, robbing you of abundance. It just isn't worth it to hang on to the past, so let God heal you by asking for the grace to forgive. This will help you to take the focus off of yourself and on to God's best will concerning you.

Ultimately, your soul must be healed of self-focus. When humankind first chose to walk away from a healthy relationship with God and to relate instead to the god of this world, lust and corruption replaced true purpose and completion. Rather than the stream of living water overflowing to others around you, your parched soul seeks any thirst-quencher the world offers. The door is opened to exile rather than the Promised Land and its corresponding opportunities and abundance.

Beth Moore tells the story of being in Angola and seeing the devastation and extreme poverty there. Although the people received seed to plant for their future needs, their hunger drove them to eat it instead. Opportunity and abundance for the future were lost. God promises that He will give seed to the sower and bread for the eater (see Isa. 55:10-11), but an unhealed soul will consume it for itself, which only leads to a soul that withers up and dies.

> Ecstasy and delight are essential to the believer's soul and they promote satisfaction. We were not meant to live without spiritual exhilaration, and the Christian who goes a long time without the experience of heart warming will soon find himself to be tempted to have his emotions satisfied from earthly things and not, as he ought, from the Sprit of God...When Christ ceases to fill the heart with satisfaction, our souls will go in silent search of other lovers. —Maurice Roberts

This 40-day fast is the time to completely focus on God, worshipping Him and laying your agenda before Him. Allow Him to heal you of self-absorption and give you a hungering and thirsting after Him that He can bless. Authentic living is a life centered on God.

> Forgiving is something that you do for yourself. It is one way of becoming the person you were created to be—and fulfilling God's dream of you is the only way to true wholeness and happiness. —Carol Luebering

Yes, today we are talking about wholeness. Wholeness represents unity, integration, congruency, interconnectedness, and completeness.

CHARACTERISTIC 7: WHOLENESS

Wholeness is living in such a way that all facets and aspects of our lives are interrelated in a physically fit, nutritionally healthy, emotionally sound, spiritually congruent, socially moral, professionally ethical, mentally resilient, and financially adept way.

Wholeness is the opposite of brokenness. When we regard our own brokenness, our natural tendency is to observe our state from a shallow perspective, excusing our habits and justifying our indifference, bitterness, competitiveness, jealousy, hatred, and prejudices, while continually shifting blame. Our modern society uses superficial and temporal terminologies to describe brokenness. We say that:

- A person breaks down when they suffer disappointment or loss.

- A person breaks focus when unable to concentrate.

- A couple breaks up when they sever relational ties.

- A person becomes broke when he or she runs out of money.

- A person's health is "broken" as a result of illness.

- Dreams are broken when they go unfulfilled.

- A train of thought is broken when interrupted.

These definitions, though descriptive, limit our perspective on brokenness to the temporal realm and, therefore, skew our understanding of what true wholeness is. The more important questions to ask that will help you move from brokenness to wholeness are:

- What is happening in the spiritual area of my life at this moment?

110

- How might God work in this time of broken-ness to restore me, renew me, remake me according to Psalm 23:5?

- Am I prepared to allow God to work in and through my current situation to bring me to greater wholeness?

These questions bring us back to the ultimate purpose of God: a total trusting belief that He is able to bring whole-ness in our lives (see 1 Thess. 5:23-24). Trusting God in this process will help you experience a new realm of spiritual empowerment.

My own experience has led me to ask myself over and over again: "What does it take to become a successful human being?" The answer: Wholeness. I've come to understand that although life may throw you curve balls, being honest and taking responsibility will help you maintain balance and a sense of wholeness. When you operate from a place of whole-ness, you strengthen your position to field any kind of ball that comes your way.

Wholeness is the fruit of God's grace working in your life. God's grace enables you to pull yourself out of the muck and mire of a world devoid of values and develop moral resilience. Faith in God allows you to live and work in a world filled with seemingly insurmountable obstacles, ambiguities, uncer-tainties, complexities, and all the other confusing aspects of life. Faith, however, requires you to accept responsibility for increasing in the knowledge of Christ so that you can tap into the grace you need to walk wholly and holy before the Lord. Wholeness requires you to accept responsibility for the decisions you make. In the final analysis, the one qual-ity that authentic people have is their willingness to take responsibility for their lives. You can only be complete if your heart is not divided between blame and unforgiveness. But when you allow faith and forgiveness to liberate and heal your soul, you will be well on your way to living on the summit of wholeness. It is God's Spirit working in you that brings healing to your heart, a sense of wholeness to your soul, and that degree of completion we are all searching for. Paul told the Colossians, *"You are complete in Him"* (Col. 2:10 NKJV).

When you are not whole, you feel insecure, ineffective, unloved, incapable, nervous, suspicious, overwhelmed, unsettled, confused, out of control, needy, isolated, lonely, and a whole host of other undesirable emotions. A whole person, on the other hand, may be challenged by circumstances, but will feel capable of handling them—largely because their relationships are healthy due to sound boundaries, honest communication, and mutual respect. Such a person practices acceptance and positive regard for others; they are not co-dependent or enmeshed in the lives of other people. Their happiness is not contingent upon how others treat them, what others say, or whether they get noticed at all.

God is a God of wholeness. He wants to bring wholeness to your life so your relationships are healthy and dynamic. Isaiah described Christ as the *"Prince of Wholeness. His ruling authority will grow, and there'll be no limits to the wholeness He brings"* (Isa. 9:6). When you cast your cares and worries on Him, as you are told to do by Paul in his letter to the Philippians, you are exchanging your brokenness for His wholeness:

> *Instead of worrying, pray. Let petitions and praises shape your worries into prayers, letting God know your concerns. Before you know it, a sense of God's wholeness, everything*

coming together for good, will come and settle you down. It's wonderful what happens when Christ displaces worry at the center of your life (Philippians 4:6).

When Christ displaces worry at the center of your life, everyone around you will know it. This is what I want you to do today.

- Identify your most pressing concerns. What causes you to lie awake at night and worry? What distracts you and causes you to furrow your brow throughout the day? Who have you allowed to chastise your peace?

- Take responsibility by shaping every irritation, offense, anxiety, or doubt into a prayer. Write down what you notice happens as a result. Who are you able to forgive? How will this affect your relationships?

Be mindful of the little things pulling at the edges of your soul. Take every thought captive as it says in Second Corinthians 10:5. It's those little foxes that spoil the garden flowering in your soul (see Song of Sol. 2:15). Practice strenuous wholeness by keeping an eye on what goes on in your soul: *"Keep your eye on the healthy soul, scrutinize the straight life; there's a future in strenuous wholeness"* (Ps. 37:37).

Nothing can cure the soul but the senses, just as nothing can cure the senses but the soul. —Oscar Wilde

May God Himself, the God who makes everything holy and whole, make you holy and whole, put you together—spirit, soul, and body—and keep you fit for the coming of our

Master, Jesus Christ. The One who called you is completely dependable. If He said it, He'll do it! (1 Thessalonians 5:23).

Day Eight

Empowering

I live in a vacuum that is as lonely as a radio tube
when the batteries are dead and there is no current
to plug in to. —Ernest Hemingway

Hemingway expresses what it feels like to be doing
life on your own. Even if you have enough talent to
get the job done, it will never accomplish all that
God intends to do if He is not your source of power. Fasting
is about removing you from the control room of your life
and realizing your absolute need for the empowering grace
of God. The good news about *the* Good News is that there
is a power source continually available to you, enabling you
to become and achieve more than you could on your own, *if*
you choose to plug into it.

According to Psalm 66, God desires to refine and purify
you like silver, the best conductor of power on Earth, so that
you become a channel of His power to do what you cannot do
alone. The question then becomes power to do what? Many
want instant growth followed quickly by instant personal
glory. E. Stanley Jones wrote, "Many want power so they can
become important through that power." However, he added,
it is only as you are linked to God's purpose that you can
expect His power. If you can surrender your own personal
agenda for God's agenda, you will be given great power to
achieve extraordinary things.

God wants to significantly change the lives of others
through ordinary people so that He is glorified. When God

gets noticed and praised, the world becomes a better place. Your ego-driven desire for the limelight clogs up your conduit of power. It actually compromises your authority rather than establishes it.

After Jesus fasted and overcame the devil, the crowds were surprised and impressed with the power of His words, that His teaching was so forthright, so confident, and so authoritative; it was not the quibbling and quoting they were used to. Jesus wasn't drawn away by their praise, but stayed focused on the will of His Father.

What would it be like if you were to walk in the power of the Spirit like Jesus did? Unexplainable results. There is a splinter in your spirit that keeps reminding you that God has more for you than you can ever imagine. Jesus said that you would do greater works than He did (see John 14:12). The Bible provides a glimpse into such a world, a world of something more—more than you can fathom or logically explain or could ever come up with on your own. A world where humans walk on water, the dead are raised to life, poisoned water is made clean, bodies are healed, captives are set free, people are transported supernaturally to another place—all accomplished by individuals who walk unhindered with the Spirit of God and are energized by a connection to divine power.

> *We pray for you all the time—pray that our God will make you fit for what He's called you to be, pray that He'll fill your good ideas and acts of faith with His own energy so that it all amounts to something* (2 Thessalonians 1:11).

Mediocrity is not part of God's definition of eternal life; authentic living is a life that is vibrant and active. The amazing part of it all is that even those things that you consider

116

ordinary become significant in God's hands. God is constantly at work, looking for ordinary people who want to partner with Him by allowing His supernatural power to be channeled through them to a hurting world.

> *The eyes of the Lord run to and fro throughout the whole earth, to show Himself strong on behalf of those whose heart is loyal to Him* (2 Chronicles 16:9 NKJV).

Be bold. Step up and get the same kind of power that the uneducated and untrained disciples of the Bible received that caused those around them to marvel when *"they realized that they had been with Jesus"* (Acts 4:13 NKJV). This 40-day fast is your time to become empowered by spending focused time with Jesus!

> Balance, peace, and joy are the fruit of a successful life. It starts with recognizing your talents and finding ways to serve others by using them. —Thomas Kinkade

One of the primary reasons for pursuing a soul fast is to regain balance in life. What is life balance? It can be hard to describe exactly. A balanced life will look different to different people. But I'm sure all will agree what it feels like when our lives are out of balance! I believe that is why many of you are reading this book. You are seeking balance.

CHARACTERISTIC 8: BALANCE

Balance, like wholeness, comes when we put our entire lives into God's hands. We begin by seeking first the Kingdom of God (see Matt. 6:33). If whatever we do, we are doing "as unto the Lord"—with a grateful heart—not seeking anything but to please God, we will find our lives naturally lining up with God's perfect will and infused by His perfect peace.

There will be hectic seasons, exhausting and trying times, but if you continue to pursue the heart of God and to be led by His Spirit, you will find constant renewal and refreshment.

I believe this is why we are told over and over throughout the Bible to do whatever we do as unto the Lord:

> *Whatever you do, whether in word or deed, do it all in the name of the Lord Jesus, giving thanks to God the Father through Him* (Colossians 3:17 NIV).

If we are first and foremost honoring God with our every thought and deed, then His peace, joy, and rest will always be near at hand. Remember, this is God's will concerning you! He wants you to "enter into His rest;" He desires for you to "rest in Him;" He has instituted the Sabbath to help you find that rest and balance in your life.

This week, I encourage you to read Hebrews 4:1-11.

- How does it feel to rest in God? peaceful

- How does it feel when you are not resting in God? hectic

Make it your number-one priority to pursue the things of God—His Word, His Spirit, His Presence. This is essential to living a balanced life. With Christ at the center, woven into every other thing you are investing time and energy in, you will naturally create a well-integrated and beautifully balanced life tapestry. If you labor at all, labor to enter into His rest! *"For he who has once entered [God's] rest also has ceased from [the weariness and pain] of human labors"* (Heb. 4:10 AMP).

Opening your whole being to be an instrument and voice from God, takes something from you as you allow God to work through you, pouring yourself out; empowerment from the Spirit is a rhythm of work and rest. —Author Unknown

Bless the Lord, oh my soul, and forget not all His benefits: who forgives all your iniquities, who heals all your diseases, who redeems your life from destruction, who crowns you with loving kindness and tender mercies, who satisfies your mouth with good things, so that your youth is renewed like the eagle's (Psalm 103:2-5 NKJV).

Day Nine

Directing

We treat (God) like a celestial aspirin that will cure headaches brought on by the steady, willful tendency of our lives away from and even against Him. We treat Him as a cosmic butler who is to clean up our messes. —Dallas Willard

Willard's description of those who simply use God to make their lives easier may sound all too familiar to you. However, as you rest from over-doing, become more mindful of God's presence, and subdue your desires by practicing the art of fasting, you will begin to see God from a new perspective. You discover an increased ability to discern and follow God's direction. The more you are able to bring your ways into alignment with His direction for authentic living, the further along you will move toward the dreams He has placed in your heart. Besides, living in opposition to God's ways won't get you anywhere:

You'll grope around in the middle of the day like a blind person feeling his way through a lifetime of darkness; you'll never get to where you're going (Deuteronomy 28:29).

Fasting tenderizes your heart, making it more like the heart of Jesus, and brings a new level of sensitivity to God's leading. God has promised that He would show you the way to go: *"I will instruct you and teach you in the way you should go; I will guide you with My eye"* (Ps. 32:8). Whether you receive God's guidance and direction through studying and reflection on His Word or He chooses to speak to you through another person, He seldom gives a written set of detailed instructions. This passage in Psalms means that God will cause you to learn what you need to know along the way. He is going to direct you as you move forward. He wants you to learn how to make choices—how to develop wisdom and discretion—just like any good father would want for his child.

Dallas Willard, in his book *Hearing God,* explains the importance of what he calls "inner directedness:"

> It is God's will that we ourselves should have a great part in determining our path through life…. A child cannot develop into a responsible, competent human being if he or she is always told what to do. Personality and character are in their very essence inner directedness…it is precisely what he wants and how he handles those wants that both reveal and make him the person he is.[1]

The good news is that as your authentic self moves to the forefront of your life your choices will become better aligned with God's purposes. There is a direct correlation between where you are now and every decision you have made in the past. Each new decision you make will determine your future. Destiny moves at the speed of decision.

In order to move into your new life, you will need to let go of some things. In his book, *The Innovation Secrets of Steve Jobs,* Carmine Gallo states, "innovation means eliminating the unnecessary so the necessary may speak." Choosing what *not* to do is as important as choosing what to do—as well as when to stop doing it. Simply because a decision was the right answer in the past doesn't mean it's the right answer now. Be willing to let go of good things if they are not in the best interest of bigger, better goals. Even an acorn must move out from under the tree where it was dropped if it ever expects to become a great oak.

It is comforting to know that God has His own dispersion process for moving the acorn to its place of destiny. Even His words contain action. Psalms 119:105 declares, *"Your word is a lamp to my feet and a light for my path"* (NKJV). This refers to much more than a beam from a flashlight on a dark trail at night. Light, like all characteristics of God, is an active, propelling energy. Scientists have actually designed spaceships with sails to take advantage of the power of light. So when the psalmist writes about light for his path, it is more like the familiar moving walkway at the airport. It propels you forward. Who knew that fasting could bring such exponential change!

> It isn't enough to talk about peace, one must believe it. And it isn't enough to believe in it, one must work for it. —Eleanor Roosevelt

As we journey toward authenticity, we are building into our lives what I am calling the 40 characteristics of an authentic person. These are the characteristics that will enable you to begin living life from the inside out—and that is what authentic living is all about.

So far this week, we have talked about the characteristics of wholeness and balance; wholeness leads to balance, and balance leads to peace!

CHARACTERISTIC 9: PEACE

If a state of peace is essential for health and prosperity to flourish in a nation, how much more in our individual lives? For this reason Paul told Timothy to pray for *"all who are in authority so that we can live peaceful and quiet lives marked by godliness and dignity"* (1 Tim. 2:2 NLT).

David instructed his young men to approach a leader from whom they sought favor with this greeting, *"Peace be to you, peace to your house, and peace to all that you have"* (1 Sam. 25:6 NKJV). Psalms states that, *"Those who love Your instructions have great peace and do not stumble"* (Ps. 119:165 NLT). And James wrote, *"Those who are peacemakers will plant seeds of peace and reap a harvest of righteousness"* (James 3:18 NLT). Jesus taught, *"Blessed are the peacemakers, for they shall be called sons of God"* (Matt. 5:9 NKJV). We all know that Jesus is the Prince of Peace, and that *"God is not the author of confusion, but of peace"* (1 Cor. 14:33 NKJV).

Take heed to the beautiful words contained in the inspirational poem written by Max Ehrmann around 1920:

> Go placidly amid the noise and haste, and remember what peace there may be in silence. As far as possible, without surrender, be on good terms with all persons. Speak your truth quietly and clearly; and listen to others, even to the dull and the ignorant, they too have their story. Avoid loud and aggressive persons, they are vexations to the spirit. Beyond a wholesome discipline, be gentle with yourself. You are a child of the universe, no less than the trees and the stars; you have a right to be here. And whether or not it is clear to you, no doubt the universe is unfolding as it should. Therefore be at peace with God, whatever you conceive Him to be, and whatever your labors and aspirations, in the noisy confusion of life, keep peace in your soul.

This week practice peace: *"Let the peace of Christ rule in your hearts, since as members of one body you were called to peace"* (Col. 3:15 NIV). How do you practice peace? How do you let the peace of Christ rule in your heart? I leave you with these instructions given by the apostle Peter:

Summing up: Be agreeable, be sympathetic, be loving, be compassionate, be humble. That goes for all of you, no exceptions. No retaliation. No sharp-tongued sarcasm. Instead, bless—that's your job, to bless. You'll be a blessing and also get a blessing.

Whoever wants to embrace life and see the day fill up with good, here's what you do: Say nothing evil or hurtful; snub evil and cultivate good; run after peace for all you're worth. God looks on all this with approval...but He turns His back on those who do evil things (1 Peter 3:8-12).

If there is light in the soul, there will be beauty in the person. If there is beauty in the person, there will be harmony in the house. If there is harmony in the house, there will be order in the nation. If there is order in the nation, there will be peace in the world. —Chinese Proverb

This core holy people will not do wrong. They won't lie, won't use words to flatter or seduce. Content with who they are and where they are, unanxious, they'll live at peace (Zephaniah 3:12-13).

Day Ten

Seeing

Prayer is reaching out after the unseen; fasting is letting go of all that is seen and temporal. Fasting helps express, deepen, confirm the resolution that we are ready to sacrifice anything, even ourselves to attain what we seek for the kingdom of God.
—Andrew Murray

You were born with an innate desire to see and explore everything—but as you grow up and are bombarded with more and more each day, you begin to unconsciously filter what you see so that it is easier to manage, and after a while, so that it fits into your preconceived ideas of the world. This is a coping mechanism we use to simplify things. It can be more comfortable to ignore whatever is inconvenient and eventually shut down to routine and habit. You get used to not noticing both the good and the bad. Your world shrinks and you start sleep-walking through life. Fasting re-energizes your senses, including your sight.

Fasting won't make difficulties disappear, but it will give you new eyes with which to see. Sometimes all you need is a fresh perspective. Who knows, maybe the answer or opportunity you are looking for is right in front of you. We are reminded of what God said through the prophets in the Book of Acts, *"I'm doing something right before your eyes that you won't believe, though it's staring you in the face"* (Acts 13:41).

SEEING WHAT OTHERS DON'T SEE

George Washington Carver was a great man of faith and an American botanical researcher and educator in the post-Civil War South. In order to restore soil from the over-planting of cotton, farmers used to plant peanuts to return nitrates to the soil. When they were harvested, though, the peanuts were simply thrown out as refuse. But couldn't something be done with this crop that would put food on the table instead of adding to the hardships of Black farmers in the South? Dr. Carver took his quandary to God. God revealed to him over 300 different uses for the peanut, making it a cash crop enabling farmers living in poverty to not only feed their families, but to prosper. "All that from a peanut?" you may ask. When some may only see a nut, people like George Washington Carver see commercial products ranging from butter to biofuel. God gave Carver new eyes to see this simple legume as the basis for hundreds of food and industrial products. As Dr. Carver so famously said, "When you do the common things in life in an uncommon way, you will command the attention of the world."

In writing about innovation, author Carmine Gallo states that creativity is simply the act of making new connections—the art of connecting things in revolutionary ways. Insight is a spiritual phenomenon. It is seeing from within—grasping what is possible from another dimension—and connecting it in some new way to your present reality. We live in a material world that co-exists with a parallel spiritual dimension—and that spiritual realm is the causal realm. What you see and experience first existed in the spirit.

Fasting gives you a greater sensitivity to that other dimension, much like putting on 3D glasses to watch a motion picture. Without the glasses, you would never know that more was going on than what your natural eyes could see. In Second Kings 6:17, Elisha prayed on behalf of his servant, *"O God, open his eyes and let him see,"* and God allowed the young man to see the chariots of fire that were protecting them in the unseen realm. King Aram, in First Kings 6, thought Elisha had placed a spy in his bedroom because Elisha knew the King's battle plans. He didn't understand that God, by His Holy Spirit, can give you spiritual eyesight to see where others cannot.

Learn to see beyond how things look. Don't trust in what you see, in your ability to interpret correctly or completely; ask God to show you opportunities and innovations He wants to bring to you and the world you impact. Tune in to Heaven's frequency so you can see through the static: *"You're blessed when you get your inside world—your mind and heart—put right. Then you can see God in the outside world"* (Matt. 5:8).

As you fast and position your soul under the supernatural power of God, you are poised to see God at work in your life and in the world around you. C.S. Lewis once said, "I believe in Christianity as I believe that the sun has risen: not only because I see it, but because by it I see everything else." Balaam's donkey saw the angels brandishing swords and standing in the way, so he ran into the ditch. Because Balaam didn't have eyes to see the unseen, he beat the donkey into continuing on the path of destruction. Fasting will help you become a detective of divinity rather than beating the donkey that is carrying you down a path God never intended for you. God wants to give you eyes to see the path to your authentic life!

> The real art of discovery consists not in finding new lands but in seeing with new eyes. —Albert Schweitzer

I've heard it said that goodness is easier to recognize than to define. Psalms tell us to *"taste and see that the Lord is good"* (Ps. 24:8). We know that God is good because of what we see Him do. James wrote that every good thing comes from the Father of lights (see James 1:17). The Father of light is the God who allows us to see what is best in every situation.

CHARACTERISTIC 10: GOODNESS

Paul posed one of the most compelling questions when he challenged the Romans:

> *You surely don't think much of God's wonderful good-ness or of His patience and willingness to put up with you. Don't you know that the reason God is good to you is because He wants you to turn to Him?* (Romans 2:4 CEV)

It is the goodness of God that leads to repentance. It is only because of God's goodness that we can have any hope of being good ourselves.

One of the most detoxifying things we can do for our souls is to turn to God and repent. This is another foundational principle and purpose of the soul fast—out with the bad and in with the good! It is a time for us to increase our capacity to *"desire and delight in...goodness"* (Hos. 6:6 AMP). When we purpose to empty ourselves of thoughts and habits that are contrary to the Spirit of Christ, and to instead fill ourselves with the knowledge of God and His ways, we become "rich in goodness." This is what Paul told the Romans: *"You yourselves are rich in goodness, amply filled with all [spiritual] knowledge"* (Rom. 15:14 AMP).

Paul told the Ephesians something similar: *"For the fruit... of the Light or the Spirit [consists] in every form of kindly goodness, uprightness of heart, and trueness of life"* (Eph. 5:9 AMP).

- Examine your life, your habits, your heart, your thoughts: Are they an expression of the life of Christ in you, "rich in goodness"?

- How would your life, habits, and thoughts be different if they consisted of "every form of goodness"?

- Think of one negative thing you can replace with something positive.

Get re-acquainted with your authentic self. Purpose to be filled with God's goodness and to express it. Become a practitioner of goodness: *"a vessel for honor, sanctified and useful for the Master, prepared for every good work"* (2 Tim. 2:21 NKJV). No matter how you sometimes look or feel, never forget who you really are:

You are royal priests, a holy nation, God's very own possession. As a result, you can show others the goodness of God, for He called you out of the darkness into His wonderful light (1 Peter 2:9 NLT).

Evil (ignorance) is like a shadow—it has no real substance of its own, it is simply a lack of light. You cannot cause a shadow to disappear by trying to fight it, stamp on it, by railing against it, or any other form of emotional or physical resistance. In order to cause a shadow to disappear, you must shine light on it. —Shakti Gawain

But all things that are exposed are made manifest by the light, for whatever makes manifest is light (Ephesians 5:13 NKJV).

Week Three

The Nature of the Soul: The Essence of You

Day Eleven

Becoming

> To deliver the soul from the sin which is its ruin
> and bestow on it the holiness which is its health
> and peace, is the end of all God's dealings with His
> children; and precisely because He cannot merely
> impose, but must enable us to attain it ourselves,
> if we are really to have the liberty of His children,
> the way He must take is long and arduous. —John
> Wood Oman[1]

When God formed humanity from the dust of the earth, as articulated in Genesis 2, He breathed into Adam and he became a living soul. The soul is that aspect of your whole being that correlates, integrates, and enlivens everything going on in the various dimensions of your self—things like your appetites, ambitions, thoughts, and motivations. It's what makes you, you. It isn't something you have, but rather who you are. C.S. Lewis is quick to clarify, "You don't have a soul. You are a Soul. You have a body."

Even though it is almost totally beyond conscious awareness, scientists have proven that the soul has real substance and weight. As you recall, it was in 1907 that a researcher by the name of Duncan MacDougall designed an experiment that documented the reality of the soul. He began by measuring animals immediately before and after their death, and found there was no difference in their weight—not surprising, because animals don't have a soul. The same experiment, however, performed on every human being he measured showed a loss of 21 grams. The scientific

135

community has embraced the fact that the soul has weight and substance.

You also have a spirit, which God intended to openly communicate with Him and rule over the soul and the body. When Adam and Eve sinned, this direct connection with God was severed, and the spirit's ability to regulate the health of soul and body was lost. This poses an enormous problem since God designed the soul to have great power: *"For as he thinketh in his heart* [soul], *so is he"* (Prov. 23:7 KJV).

When the spirit, soul, and body are out of order, you become governed by exterior forces rather than the inner stream of God's Living Water—*"the life-giving Spirit of God"* (Isa. 11:1). You lose the ability to discern your authentic self. What you allow to govern your soul will ultimately determine what you receive from God. As God spoke through the prophet Jeremiah, *"I the Lord search the mind, I try the heart, even to give to every man according to his ways"* (Jer. 17:9 AMP).

Sin is certainly one of the factors God is looking for in your heart. But He can only bless you in proportion to the condition of your soul. Are your feelings and emotions roadblocks to His work in your life? It isn't that God won't bless you, but that He can't bless you until your soul is rightly ordered and restored to God's original plan.

The incredible good news is that God desires your soul to prosper—to rise to the highest level of existence that He worked into your being when He formed you in the womb. The apostle John wrote, *"Beloved, I pray that you may prosper in all things and be in health, just as your soul prospers"* (3 John 1:2 NKJV).

We'll cover your thought life in a later chapter, but during this time of fasting, we will focus on restoring, resting, imaging, and sensing as divine disciplines regarding the nature of—and plan for—your soul.

> The main purpose of life is to live rightly, think rightly, act rightly. The soul must languish when we give all our thought to the body. —Mohandas Gandhi

Another primary reason for pursuing a 40-day fast is to develop the characteristic of discipline. You will need to exercise the art of discipline if you are to master the art of living authentically.

CHARACTERISTIC 11: DISCIPLINE

Paul emphasized the importance of discipline in almost every letter he wrote. In the Book of Acts he said, *"I always exercise and discipline myself...to have a clear (unshaken, blameless) conscience, void of offense toward God and toward men"* (Acts 24:16 AMP).

He told Timothy to *"exercise daily in God—no spiritual flabbiness, please! Workouts in the gymnasium are useful, but a disciplined life in God is far more so, making you fit both today and forever"* (1 Tim. 4:8-9). Then, in his next letter to Timothy, he reassured him with this statement: *"God has not given us a spirit of fear and timidity, but of power, love, and self-discipline"* (2 Tim. 1:7 NLT).

Peter also wrote about discipline: *"So don't lose a minute in building on what you've been given, complementing your basic faith with...alert discipline"* (2 Pet. 1:5).

So how do we exercise a disciplined life in God? Is it simply a matter of following a rigid daily routine or denying ourselves our favorite foods? Paul said the discipline of God is not so much about what we choose *not* to do, but more about what we choose *to* do. He warned against the dangers of legalism and admonished seekers to focus instead on the law of love.

A disciplined life in God will produce the fruit of the Spirit: *"love, joy, peace, patience, kindness, goodness, faithfulness, gentleness, and self-control"* (Gal. 5:22-23 NLT). Paul explained it to the Colossians like this:

> *So, chosen by God for this new life of love, dress in the wardrobe God picked out for you: compassion, kindness, humility, quiet strength, discipline. Be even-tempered, content with second place, quick to forgive an offense. Forgive as quickly and completely as the Master forgave you. And regardless of what else you put on, wear love. It's your basic, all-purpose garment. Never be without it* (Colossians 3:12-14).

These are the disciplines of the soul I want you to focus on this week. Practice *"taking every thought captive to the obedience of Christ"* (2 Cor. 10:5 NASB)—that means every unloving, unforgiving, selfish thought!

Reinforce your victories! Each day write down an instance you chose to think a loving thought instead of an unloving one. Keep it up until loving thoughts become a habit.

> Moral excellence comes about as a result of habit. We become just by doing just acts, temperate by doing temperate acts, brave by doing brave acts.
> —Aristotle

Get out there and walk—better yet, run—on the road God called you to travel. ...Do this with humility and discipline—not in fits and starts, but steadily, pouring yourselves out for each other in acts of love (Ephesians 4:1-3).

Day Twelve

Restoring

If only Christians would live according to their belief in the teaching of Jesus we all would become Christians. —Mahatma Gandhi

Why is it that so many Christians aren't living the abundant life? I believe it has to do with the incongruence of what they profess to believe with what they are actually convinced of. What you believe to be true in the depths of your soul is played out in your mind, translated through your will, and made evident by your emotions. As Paul told the Romans, *"You're fortunate if your behavior and your belief are coherent"* (Rom. 14:22). That coherency determines how authentically you live and how healthy your soul is.

The key to restoring your soul is bringing that congruency to every dimension of your life. Where is there a breakdown between what you believe and how you behave—the Word in your heart versus the words that come out of your mouth? Is the kingdom within you divided?

Jesus said, *"The Kingdom of God is within you"* (Luke 17:21 NKJV). I think of a vast territory where unlimited natural resources lie buried, but because the country is underdeveloped, the infrastructure is not sufficient to extract and export them, so they aren't of any benefit. Or there is internal conflict so that roads are blocked and communication lines are down. How does the geography of your soul look? Do you need to establish order, repair the power lines, or just mend some fences?

An entire kingdom resides within the borders of your soul. You are the one who determines which forces will reign there—you alone are captain and defender of the realm.

Think of the soul as a living cell having a wall of protection designed to filter what gets in—ideally, only allowing information that is aligned with truth to enter and rejecting all deception. However, because your soul is intended to receive sustenance from the Spirit of God and His Word, when the soul is cut off from this central power source, the permeable wall erodes allowing falsehoods to enter like weeds or wild bandits that bring corruption and chaos.

Furthermore, the pain inflicted by others must get metabolized or things like envy, bitterness, and unforgiveness will penetrate and poison your soul, leading to disease. These toxins will break down the integrity of your soul, leading to disorder and confusion. When the boundaries of the soul cease to function correctly, egocentric self-protection takes over shutting down your ability to receive new ideas, including new strategies that God wants to give you.

King David once cried out to the Lord that his soul was cast down and in despair. Author Phillip Keller, himself a shepherd, said that it is a pathetic sight to see a "cast" sheep that has rolled over onto its back, feet in the air, frantically struggling. The sheep is down and can't get up. Keller explains that it is the fat, comfort-seeking sheep that lies down and then finds its center of gravity has shifted. Sheep with too much wool, he says, can also become heavily matted with mud, manure, and other debris and find themselves incapacitated. The life-giving blood supply then becomes cut off by gases that build up in the stomach. Buzzards circle overhead, waiting for the sure death that will eventually come.

David wrote in Psalm 23 that the Lord was a good shepherd who would surely restore and set upright his soul. "*The Lord is my shepherd…. He restores my soul*" (Ps. 23:1,3 NKJV). If you allow Him during this time of fasting, God will remove the mud and debris clogging your soul and keeping you cast down. The enemy is prowling about, looking for one who is down and can't get up, but God with His watchful eye sees you and wants to restore you—your creative power, your wisdom, your intuition—and put you back on the cutting edge of life. He wants to reconnect you to your soul's nourishment—the Spirit of God—and the power and capacity that are beyond anything you could achieve on your own.

The word *restore* implies putting something back, to reestablish, or bring back to a previous state. The question to ask is: "Back to what?" When God created Adam and the rest of creation, He placed Adam in the Garden and declared it was good—"of use, of benefit." Adam was righteous before God. The word *righteous*, according to *Strong's Concordance*, means "he who is as he ought to be." Adam was as he was designed to be. After sin entered the scene, there were none righteous, "*not even one…all have become useless*" (see Rom. 3:10-18 NLT). Humankind became bent toward sin; habits, thoughts, and feelings were all inclined toward self and away from God and others. Spirit, soul, and body became divided and lacked integration. In redeeming you, God is restoring your bent toward the oughtness of your authentic self. Your spirit again becomes a place where living water freely flows.

God has fearfully and wonderfully made you. The Garden is now intended to be in you rather than you in the Garden. "*In simple humility let our gardener, God, landscape you with the Word, making a salvation-garden of your life*" (James 1:21).

The way to gain a good reputation is to endeavor to
be what you desire to appear. —Socrates

Almost more than anything else, the soul fast should help
us clear and restore our minds lest they be *"corrupted from the
simplicity that is in Christ"* (2 Cor. 11:3 NKJV).

CHARACTERISTIC 12: SIMPLICITY

The 40 days of Lent, as with any fast, are a period of time
set aside for keeping the main thing the main thing—for
focusing on what is important in our lives as children of God.
As Paul told the Galatians: *"What is important is faith expressing
itself in love"* (Gal. 5:6 NLT).

It's so important that we don't get distracted by "dos" and
"don'ts," but rather the power of hoping and believing in
Christ as evidenced by our love for one another. This alone
is how we "vigilantly guard our souls"—it is by our "love of
God" (see Josh. 23:11-13). And Jesus taught there is but one
proof of our love of God. He said, *"All will know that you are
My disciples, if you have love for one another"* (John 13:35 NKJV).

The Bible states over and over that it is not sacrifice, but
obedience the Lord seeks—and that obedience is demonstrated by our love walk. We know we are led of the Spirit
when we choose love. *"Love is the fulfillment of the law"* (Rom.
13:10 NKJV). How much simpler could it be? Peter said it this
way: *"You have purified your souls in obeying the truth through the
Spirit in sincere love of the brethren, love one another fervently with a
pure heart"* (1 Pet. 1:22 NKJV).

There is no more nourishing and detoxifying soul food
than love. Ecclesiastes says, *"We work to feed our appetites; mean-
while our souls go hungry"* (Eccles. 6:7). Today, feed your soul

144

by pursuing the simplicity demonstrated by Christ—demonstrate love. You cultivate or nourish your soul in this arena by doing this one simple thing: *"Keep your minds on whatever is true, pure, right, holy, friendly, and proper. Don't ever stop thinking about what is truly worthwhile and worthy of praise"* (Phil. 4:8 CEV).

Do this *"in simplicity of purpose...because of your reverence for the Lord and as a sincere expression of your devotion to Him"* (Col. 3:22 AMP).

Keep it simple. Walk in love. This is how you will uncover your authentic self, created in the image of love*: "it's the rich simplicity of being yourself before God"* (1 Tim. 6:6). Just be yourself before God, for God loves you just as you are! And being yourself before Him is how you can love Him in return. Love being yourself.

I leave you today with these instructions from Jesus as recorded in the Matthew:

> *Here's what I want you to do: Find a quiet, secluded place so you won't be tempted to role-play before God. Just be there as simply and honestly as you can manage. The focus will shift from you to God, and you will begin to sense His grace* (Matthew 6:6).

True religion is real living; living with all one's soul, with all one's goodness and righteousness. —Albert Einstein

Day Thirteen

Resting

To have a quiet mind is to possess one's mind wholly; to have a calm spirit is to possess one's self.
—Hamilton Wright Mabie

Your soul was designed to keep pace with God, walking in a rhythm of going out and coming into a place of rest. A body that isn't rested demands to be heard, ego craves greater power, and increasing passions and appetites begin to rule the soul. Stress causes the adrenal glands to release the hormone cortisol, which produces concentration and memory problems. Even work done for God can overload your system so you become weak and lose focus. The demands of work and the world system can be oppressive and enslave you by all types of bondage. The more you do, the more is demanded of you so that you become trapped in a vicious cycle that God didn't intend.

Listen to what Jesus invites you to instead:

Are you tired? Worn out? Burned out on religion? Come to Me. Get away with Me and you'll recover your life. I'll show you how to take a real rest. Walk with Me and work with Me—watch how I do it. Learn the unforced rhythms of grace. I won't lay anything heavy or ill-fitting on you. Keep company with Me and you'll learn to live freely and lightly (Matthew 11:28-30).

The Sabbath and sleep are two types of rest instituted by God as part of the rhythm of His creation—like the cadence of ocean waves, the rotation of the planets, and the beating of a human heart. Rhythm has purpose. Similar to the dissonance you feel when clapping off beat to the rhythm of music, your soul experiences a tension when rest doesn't come in regular cycles.

Sleep and rest were ordained by God because He is a God of balance. As the sun goes down every night and the tides go out every evening, all life was designed to ebb and flow and pulse and beat rhythmically. As Isaac Newton discovered, for every action, there is always an equal and opposite reaction. So it is with the life of your soul. It must become quiet and still in order to be fortified and renewed. Sleep is the time when memory of the day's events is filtered and solidified. Connections in the brain are reinforced so that you receive the benefit of what you did without having to repeat the learning again tomorrow. Scientists believe deep sleep is as important to strengthening your skills as what you do while you are awake. You are increased while you sleep.

The Sabbath provides access to the inner rhythm of creation itself, where the soul can be weaned from the world's control and mentored by God. It is a time to be your true self; not a role you play. There is great mystery in ceasing to do and yet accomplishing more. That is what God promises He will do through you—if, that is, you are willing to trust He can run the universe without you. Are you willing to stop trying long enough to let Him?

> *If you watch your step on the Sabbath and don't use My holy day for personal advantage, if you treat the Sabbath as a day of joy, God's holy day as a celebration, if you honor it by refusing "business as usual," making money, running here and there—then you'll be free to enjoy God!*

148

Oh, I'll make you ride high and soar above it all (Isaiah 58:13-14).

If you can loosen your grip on your life, God will lift you up and cause you to *"ride high and soar above it all."* God wants to give you well-furnished houses you didn't buy, wells you didn't dig, and vineyards and olive orchards you didn't plant (see Deut. 6:11). That's the kind of high place, soul rest, and inheritance that comes from being in the stream of God's will for your life. Don't be like the Israelites of old who refused:

Stand by the ways and see and ask for the ancient paths, where the good way is, and walk in it; and you will find rest for your souls (Jeremiah 6:16 NASB).

We often spend so much time coping with problems along our path that we only have a dim or even inaccurate view of what's really important to us. —Peter Senge

Your soul is what makes you uniquely you. Your soul is imprinted with an eternally unique DNA that holds within it the keys to your purpose, potential, and destiny. I say "eternally unique" because nobody in the history of the world has ever been—or ever will be—just like you.

CHARACTERISTIC 13: UNIQUENESS

Once upon a time there was a crooked tree and a straight tree. They grew up alongside of each other. Every day the straight tree would look at the crooked tree and say, "You're crooked. You've always been crooked and you'll continue to be crooked. But look at me! I'm tall and I'm straight." And then one day, the lumberjacks came into the forest, looked around, and the manager in charge said, "Cut all the straight trees." And that crooked tree is still there to this day, growing strong and growing strange.[1]

God is a God of originality. Even nature testifies of this. When snowflakes fall, they travel through various layers of the atmosphere and endure different kinds of temperature combined with varying degrees of velocity. Although they are born from the same source, no two are alike when they finally hit the Earth. You are a one-of-a-kind expression of God's glory. The divine essence of you is a mold-breaking product that is being conveyed in a unique package with a distinctive logo and branding exclusively your own. You are God's unique expression of Himself in the Earth realm.

As the psalmist, David, proclaimed, *"I will praise You, for I am fearfully and wonderfully made; marvelous are Your works, and that my soul knows very well"* (Ps. 139:14 NKJV). Inspired by Psalm 145, liturgical composer, Juliana Howard, penned, "Let Your glory within me shine out to the world."

Today, I want you to stir up the unique expression of God's glory and grace He has woven into your soul—the divine essence of your being. Call out and celebrate those things that make you uniquely you:

- List five aspects of your personality that make you special.

- List five desires that are uniquely yours.

- List five strengths that you bring to the table.

- List five talents that God has given you to steward.

150

Take time to praise God for the magnificent tapestry that makes you who you are—stop and celebrate the wonder that is *you* and glorify God for your uniqueness. *"This is the* [person] *the Lord has made; let us rejoice and be glad!"* (Ps. 118:24 NASB). Be grateful for the gift God created you to be! Rejoice in the wonder and majesty that is you.

> *You shaped me first inside, then out; You formed me in my mother's womb. ...Body and soul, I am marvelously made! ...What a creation! You know me inside and out, You know every bone in my body; You know exactly how I was made, bit by bit, how I was sculpted from nothing into something. Like an open book, You watched me grow...the days of my life all prepared before I'd even lived one day* (Psalm 139:13-16).

To have a firm persuasion in our work—to feel that what we do is right for ourselves and good for the world at the same exact time—is one of the great triumphs of human existence. —David Whyte

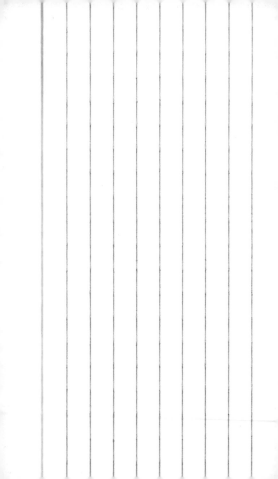

Day Fourteen

Imaging

The noble man is only God's image. —Ludwig Tieck

Genesis chapter 1 says that human beings are made in the image of God. Second Peter chapter 1 tells us each individual is formed with divine, creative potential. Theologians have debated for hundreds of years what "made in the image" might look like. It could certainly be said that it has to do with how people and God are similar—qualities such as being loving, generous, and compassionate. Although Adam was not a god, he was nonetheless very much like God. So you, too, were created to be like Him. However, being created in His image means more than just being similar to God—it means being created with His very nature and DNA.

Genesis says that God blessed Adam and Eve, telling them to be fruitful and multiply, and "fill the earth, and subdue it; and rule over" it. Psalm 8 declares that man was made *a little lower than God*" and that God has made him to rule over the works of His hands putting *"all things under his feet."* That's a pretty tall order for human beings, no matter what their gifts and talents.

It is God's intent that you are to represent Him on this Earth, to image Him wherever you are. The word *rule* means "to govern, manage, or steward," implying that you are to carry out the wishes of another. It also involves the idea of having the authority to act on behalf of someone else. One author says that you are to establish an outpost on God's behalf, very similar to the idea of an embassy on foreign soil.

God wants to give you power to activate your authority to do great things for Him. It will necessitate a soul—a mind, will, and emotions—fully conformed to the image of Christ so that the picture you present to the world is an accurate representation of Him. When Jesus was leaving this Earth He told the disciples in Acts 1 that they would receive power and were to be His witnesses—they were to represent Him, act on His behalf, and show others what He looked like, just as He showed the world what God the Father looks like.

Nothing is a better representation of God than a vibrant life. Saint Irenaeus, a church father in the second century, said, "The glory of God is man fully alive." Encountering a lush, green oasis in the middle of a hot, dry desert doesn't take a genius to realize that something is different—there is life there, not artificial turf. When you live authentically, you evidence the life of Christ. How you act toward others reflects your progress toward that end. Andrew Murray said, "Our humility toward others is the only sufficient proof that our humility before God is real."

What an amazing thought that God has chosen to work through mere human beings—vessels of clay—knowing all their weaknesses and vulnerabilities. Yet the Bible says the work doesn't depend upon you, but upon God who promises that in your weakness He will be strong. Dream big, knowing that through you God will reveal Himself—and in doing so, your own true self will be revealed. After all, you were made in His image, made to reflect His likeness, to manifest His glory. Believe what God said about who He is and who you are in relation to Him. John wrote that, "*whoever...believed He was who He claimed and would do what He said, He made to be their true selves, their child-of-God selves"* (John 1:12). Have you ever seriously thought about what it means to be God's offspring? To be imprinted with His DNA? What does the God gene in you look like?

I believe God will reveal more of how He has imprinted you with Himself; especially in the areas you are most weak, as you yield to what He shows you during this 40-day soul fast.

According to Romans 8, all creation is waiting to see who you will become!

> If I were to wish for anything, I should not wish for wealth and power, but for the passionate sense of the potential, for the eye which, ever young and ardent, sees the possible. Pleasure disappoints, possibility never. —Søren Kierkegaard

Yesterday we talked about the importance of embracing your uniqueness. Today I want to talk to you about the importance of embracing your passions. It is passion that gives you eyes to see what is possible and the fortitude to pursue it. Passion will cause you to take risks and stand against the odds: *"God's holy people passionately and faithfully stand their ground"* (Rev. 13:10).

CHARACTERISTIC 14: PASSION

Your passions are those things that drive you to do and be more—those things that make you feel alive, cause you to forget limiting circumstances or perceived shortcomings, and enable you to feel the joy of doing something beyond yourself—sometimes you forget the "self" in pursuit of such passions.

The things you are passionate about are God-given desires. God's desires in you will move you out of the egocentric, self-centered realm you would otherwise occupy. They cause you to live on a higher plane and tap into the dimension of supernatural ability and resources.

When you are in the passionate pursuit of something, you connect with the mind of God and His creativity. Passion is the driving force of purpose and the fuel you'll need to maximize your potential.

Passion will stir the desire within you to advance in a particular discipline, field, or industry. Paul, who accomplished more than anyone else in Church history, wrote to the Corinthians about *"the passion of God burning inside me"* (2 Cor. 11:1).

Your passions are embedded in the DNA of your soul. Along with your intrinsic desires, proclivities, temperament, and objectives. *"You, Lord, Who know all hearts (their thoughts, passions, desires, appetites, purposes, and endeavors)"* (Acts 1:24 AMP). Your inherent passions are part of your genetic makeup.

- What are you passionate about?

- How can you harness the power of your passions to establish yourself, take dominion, and stand your ground?

Take a few minutes to ponder this and journal what comes to mind.

I want to encourage you with Paul's words to the Corinthians: *"You do so well in so many things—you trust God, you're articulate, you're insightful, you're passionate, you love—now go and do your best"* (2 Cor. 8:7).

How can you tap into your passions to "go and do your best?"

You're more alive, more concerned, more sensitive, more reverent, more human, more passionate, more responsible. Looked at from any angle, you've come out of this with purity of heart (2 Corinthians 7:11).

Leadership is the capacity to influence others through inspiration generated by a passion ignited by a purpose. True leadership has very little to do with what you do and is fundamentally a matter of who you are. True leadership is self-discovery. True leadership is the impact of one's commitment to self-manifestation. —Myles Munroe

When work, commitment, and pleasure all become one and you reach that deep well where passion lives, nothing is impossible. —Nancy Coey

Day Fifteen

Sensing

The subconscious mind is more susceptible to influence by impulses of thought mixed with "feeling" or emotion than by those originating solely in the reasoning portion of the mind.
—Napoleon Hill

The parable of the Good Samaritan is a well-known passage of Scripture found in Luke 10. In the story, three men encounter the same wounded man lying on the side of a road, but only one is moved to act on behalf of the injured party. It would be easy to miss one of the distinguishing factors between the three men. The Samaritan, we are told, *"when he saw him, he felt compassion"* (Luke 10:33 NASB). Feelings move you, like the Samaritan, to action, either positively or negatively.

The will is controlled by the mind and its emotions, which if properly ordered can compel us to do heroic things. We can't assume in the story that the priest or the Levite simply had no feelings. They could have felt fear or condescension or a basic urgency to get to where they were going. The point of Jesus' narrative was not to consider their feelings, but to point out that what they felt was out of order—it ruled over the right thing to do.

Disaster happens when your soul becomes organized around feelings. A negative feeling or prevailing mood can spread into your whole life; like a red towel in a load of white clothes—it bleeds on everything. The mind then joins in by defending the feeling, looking for justification, and finally ceasing to think rationally. But even negative emotions and feelings like anger, fear, and frustration can be helpful flags to let you know that there is work to be done in your soul or in your relationships.

God created you to sense, to feel, to have impressions. Paul said in Philippians 3:10 that he desired to know the fellowship of the suffering of Jesus, meaning he wanted to sense what He sensed—both pain and joy. The body, mind, and spirit all have the ability to experience sensations and glean from the world—both the seen and unseen. God gave you emotions that would incline you to enjoy participating in life—as well as to turn you away from desires that could keep you in bondage and morph into full-blown lusts. Feelings can draw you closer to God and compel you to do good—or distract you.

The key isn't to deny or repress your feelings—but to control them. God wants to help you reorder your spirit, soul, and body so that you can effectively discern and manage what you are feeling. God desires to restore your emotions, replacing them with positive feelings associated with love, joy, and peace—and heal the negative images and lying interpretations that satan whispers in your ear about who you are and who God is. A positive emotional experience brings hope and healing—but when the enemy perverts those emotions in a negative way, they bring despair and destruction.

In today's world, people go to all kinds of extremes just to feel anything. This generation has more choices about what to do than any generation before and often has no clue how to decide what is good or healthy for the soul.

Without a clear direction in life, whatever offers the greatest sensation becomes the basis for making decisions.

A wealthy Tolstoy describes a time in his life when lack of purpose accompanied by excess brought his life to a complete standstill. It wasn't that he was misguided by wrong feelings, since he really had no strong feelings. "There was no life, for there were no wishes I could consider reasonable. Had a fairy come and offered to fulfill my desires I should not have known what to ask." Then Tolstoy met some hard-working Russian peasants who had a firmer grasp on the meaning of life and true convictions about what they felt; it changed his life forever.

Filter through what you feel—or don't feel—and listen for what those cues are telling you. Are you masking some deeper feelings by allowing what may be "habitual feelings" to dictate who you are, how you react, what you do? Examine your emotional patterns—do you react in certain ways out of habit? Ask God to help you look deeper and harness your truest feelings—practice sensing what brings you most joy. Try to feel what God feels in any given situation—whether it is compassion, sadness, or ecstasy. Tuning into what moves you, grieves you, or elates you will increase your capacity to live more authentically.

> Learning to live in the present moment is part of the path of joy. Begin today. Declare out loud to the universe that you are willing to let go of struggle and eager to learn through joy. —Sarah Ban Breathnach

The characteristic of joy—and joyfulness—is one of the most, if not *the* most, significant and telling traits of an authentic person. It demonstrates, as well as determines, successful authentic living in so many ways.

CHARACTERISTIC 15: JOY

The Bible says, *"The joy of the Lord is your strength and strong-hold"* (Neh. 8:10 AMP). Without joy, you can't be strong. Your soul won't be healthy. You will be rendered weak and vulnerable. Being joy-deprived is similar to, if not worse than, being sleep-deprived!

Whenever the enemy steals your joy—and therefore your peace—he emaciates you and breaks down your emotional immune system, leaving you vulnerable to attack.

The Kingdom of God can only reign within you in all *"righteousness and peace and joy in the Holy Spirit"* (Rom. 14:17 NKJV). And remember that *"righteousness is sown in peace by those who make peace"* (James 3:18 NKJV)—so you can't walk in the fruit of righteousness without peace. And you can't walk in peace without joy!

Joy precedes peace in the lineup of spiritual fruit presented in Galatians 5:22: *"the fruit of the Spirit is love, joy, peace"* (NKJV). We have talked a great deal about the importance of walking in love in order to living more authentically. But now we see that according to Galatians 5:22, the first expression of love is the fruit of joy. It is almost impossible not to be loving when you are brimming over with joy. Joyfulness makes all of the other spiritual fruit flow effortlessly. It empowers you to be your most divine self.

Jesus told His disciples that all He had taught them was so that His joy might remain in them, and that their joy might be full (see John 15:11). Joy is important. Peter stated that, *"yet believing, you rejoice with joy inexpressible and full of glory"* (1 Pet. 1:8 NKJV). Again, Jesus reiterated, *"Ask, and you will receive, that your joy may be full"* (John 16:24 NKJV). And Paul instructed that no matter what, *"be full of joy in the Lord. I say it again—rejoice!"* (Phil. 4:4 NLT).

- How can you stir up joy in your everyday life?

- What can you do to eliminate those things that would steal your joy?

Jesus came to empower you to maximize your joy because joy is your key to victory and a more vibrant and satisfying life. Joy is not only healing and restorative, but it is a powerful spiritual force. Jesus sought to teach you how to harness the raw power of simple joy. As the author and finisher of our faith, Jesus tapped into the power of joy to enable Him to endure the Cross (see Heb. 12:2). Now that's powerful.

> What was once impossible now summons us to dismantle the walls between ourselves and our sisters and brothers, to dissolve the distinctions between flesh and spirit, to transcend the present limits of time and matter, to find, at last, not wealth or power but the ecstasy (so long forgotten) of commonplace, unconditional being. For the atom's soul is nothing but energy. Spirit blazes in the dullest of clay. The life of every woman or man—the heart of it—is pure and holy joy. —George B. Leonard

> If the sight of the blue skies fills you with joy, if a blade of grass springing up in the fields has power to move you, if the simple things in nature have a message you understand, rejoice, for your soul is alive. —Eleanora Duse

May the God of hope fill you with all joy and peace in believing, that you may abound in hope by the power of the Holy Spirit (Romans 15:13 NKJV).

Week Four

The Properties of Thought: You Are What You Think

Day Sixteen

Believing

All that a man achieves or fails to achieve is a direct result of his own thoughts. —James Allen

The theory that conscious thought impacts matter is not any secret, nor is it "new age." James Allen was publishing articles about the power of thought in the late 1800s—his first book, *From Poverty to Power* was published in 1901, and his most famous work, *As a Man Thinketh* became a bestseller in 1903. During this same period, Andrew Carnegie, the mid-nineteenth century captain of industry, was retiring from his own rise from poverty to power to research and write *The Law of Success,* which he did in collaboration with Napoleon Hill. This was a precursor to the idea most people know now as "The Law of Attraction." It wasn't until twelve years later, in 1937, that Napoleon Hill published his now-classic, *Think and Grow Rich,* in which he details countless cases of well-known men who changed their lives and accumulated great wealth simply by changing their thought life.

Today, quantum physicists tell us that nothing in the universe is static, but instead all is vibrating energy. They call this String Theory. They go on to purport that this vibrating energy responds to the vibrations of human thought, substantiating the theory that you attract what you think. Princeton physicist John A. Wheeler confirms that subjective consciousness and objective matter mutually create each other.

Understanding there is scientifically measurable power to your thoughts shouldn't be so hard to believe for those of us who have grown up hearing about the power of faith. Jesus said that, *"It shall be done for you as you have believed"* (Matt. 8:13 AMP) and that, *"All things are possible to him who believes"* (Mark 9:23 NASB). Jesus is talking about the sheer power of belief— the power of your thoughts to impact your reality. This truth is based in the teachings of the Torah. Proverbs 23:7 states, *"For as he thinks within himself, so he is"* (NASB).

As powerful as your thoughts are to change your life, changing your thinking can be extremely difficult. Your pre-existing assumptions about the world that you live in and the ideas and images planted in your subconscious mind determine what you are able to see, hear, and otherwise perceive. They set boundaries on what you are able and willing to do. Who you believe you are and what you think you are capable of doing are determining factors in accomplishing your destiny, but so is your belief about how this world operates. When Jesus said, *"Whatever you bind on earth will be bound in heaven, and whatever you loose on earth will be loosed in heaven"* (Matt. 18:18 NKJV), or instructed us to pray that what is done in Heaven will also be done on the Earth (see Matt. 6:10), only small glimpses are given in Scripture of what that actually means. Former Archbishop of Canterbury, William Temple, once said, "We only know what Matter is when Spirit dwells in it; we only know what Man is when God dwells in him."[1] The Spirit of God is the life force of which everything consists. We see and understand by that Spirit when we are willing to look through the lens of Scripture. Even then, we can only know what we are willing to believe.

Your thoughts are all of the ways you are conscious of reality—they form your reality—your memories, beliefs, ideas, and images. Most of these ways of knowing reside so deeply in you that it is hard to tell which may be affecting your life. You will never have more or go farther or accomplish greater things than your thoughts will allow you to. But as quickly as light illuminates a room, a single thought can shed new light on your life, changing everything including your destiny. The Gospel entering your heart empowers you to become a full participant in God's Kingdom which is present on Earth— within you—right now, and available to you if you are willing to open your mind to new ways of thinking and seeing.

Your life moves in the direction of your thoughts, like a current moving you either closer or farther away from your best destiny. If you want to change your life, you must begin by changing your thoughts. *"Let this mind be in you which was also in Christ Jesus"* (Phil. 2:5 NKJV). This verse is just as mind-boggling as String Theory when you consider the things that Jesus did while in a human body and with a human mind. A whole universe of possibilities is waiting to be released through you from the Creator God. Physicist Jack Sarfatti noted, "The possibilities of physical matter are to be fully revealed only from the mind of its Maker,"[2] and only, according to the Gospel of Mark, *"If you can believe, all things are possible"* (Mark 9:23 NKJV).

Changing your thinking is about receiving, focusing, envisioning, and conquering—four practices we will be focusing on throughout the remainder of this week.

Worship is the submission of all of our nature to God. It is the quickening of conscience by His holiness, nourishment of mind by His truth, purifying of imagination by His beauty, opening of the heart to His love, and submission of will to His purpose. And all this gathered up in adoration is the greatest of human expressions of which we are capable. —Archbishop William Temple

One of the most compelling reasons for journeying toward authenticity is to uncover the genuine beauty of your truest self. It is a process of peeling away the layers of artificial roles we so often play and the lies and limitations we so often impose on our own souls.

CHARACTERISTIC 16: BEAUTY

You, the real you, is a work of art. A masterpiece. When I think of cultivating "beauty of soul," I think of a soul's originality, vibrancy, and richness—awe-provoking intricacy and complexity of color—great depths and heights of potential and the human soul's immense capacity to reflect God's glory.

Your soul is beautiful if for no other reason than it was created to express the divine magnificence of the Creator. Jesus said:

> *If God gives such attention to the appearance of wildflowers—most of which are never even seen—don't you think He'll attend to you, take pride in you, do His best for you?* (Matthew 6:30)

In other words, stop striving. Stop fussing. Relax in the beautiful you God created you to be and worship Him in that beauty.

Jesus followed that thought with this statement, *"What I'm trying to do here is to get you to relax, to not be so preoccupied with getting so you can respond to God's giving"* (Luke 12:29).

Think about that for a moment.

170

- What would it look like to relax and "respond to God's giving"—to simply *"Be still and rest in the Lord; wait for Him and patiently lean yourself upon Him; fret not yourself"* (Ps. 37:7 AMP)? What kind of a beauty treatment would that be for your soul?

Create space in your life for a spiritual beauty spa. Soak in God's presence. Allow God's Spirit to wash away any impurities, to peel away the old, dead things and soften the rough places. *"Worship the Lord in the beauty of holiness"* (Ps. 96:9 NKJV). And like David, say to the Lord, *"I shall be satisfied when I awake in Your likeness"* (Ps. 17:15 NKJV).

This is true beauty: the beauty of holiness—the beauty of wholeness—the beauty of living in communion with God. This beauty comes from deep within—from *"the hidden person of the heart, with the incorruptible beauty of a gentle and quiet spirit, which is very precious in the sight of God"* (1 Pet. 3:4 NKJV).

Today, focus on cultivating authentic beauty.

Insomuch as love grows in you, so in you beauty grows. For love is the beauty of the soul. —St. Augustine

One thing I have desired of the Lord, that will I seek: that I may...behold the beauty of the Lord, and to inquire in His temple (Psalm 27:4).

Day Seventeen

Receiving

To the individual believer, who is, by the very fact of relationship to Christ, indwelt by the Holy Spirit of God, there is granted the direct impression of the Spirit of God on the Spirit of man, imparting the knowledge of His will in matters of the smallest and greatest importance. This has to be sought and waited for. —G. Campbell Morgan[1]

God desires to communicate with ordinary human beings and to impart His love and blessing through them. Simply because you don't hear doesn't mean He isn't speaking. Messages available to radios, computers, telephones, and televisions are always passing through the atmosphere, but an appropriate receiver is required to make use of them. You must believe that such unseen signals are available to you and will provide worthwhile information and life-changing new ideas. When Adam fell, he fell lost the full capacity for communicating with God—for tuning into His spiritual bandwidth. He went from a satellite type of communication to AM type communication, from fiber-optics/digital to analog.

If you want to progress in life, you have to think progressive thoughts, and the best place to receive them from is the Creator. But don't be surprised if you encounter resistance from people confined by preconceived analog-assumptions limited by what they've only known before now. Be willing to shift your paradigm even when those around you are not.

That is how game-changing innovation happens and life-altering spiritual technologies discoveries are made.

Guglielmo Marconi dreamed of a system for harnessing the intangible forces of the unseen world. When he told his friends he had discovered a principle that would enable him to send messages through the air, without the aid of wires or other direct physical means of communication, they insisted he undergo a psychological evaluation. He went on to win a Nobel Prize in Physics for his contributions to the development of wireless telegraphy.

Do you need a new product for your business? A new insight for your marriage or your ministry? Are you ready for God to open the doors of opportunity to take you to the next level in your career? There are treasures hidden in Creation since the beginning of time that God is going to reveal through a human being who is asking, knocking, and seeking; who is ready to obey; and who will give Him the glory for the results.

> *Yes, if you call out for insight and raise your voice for understanding, if you seek it like silver and search for it as for hidden treasures, then you will understand the fear of the Lord and find the knowledge of God* (Proverbs 2:3-5 ESV).

Adam and Eve spoke directly with God in the cool of the evening as they walked in the Garden. But after the Fall, the minds of humans were veiled, separating their minds from the truth and reality of God's perspective. Today, says C.S. Lewis, "God walks everywhere incognito." He chooses when to reveal Himself—when to pull back the veil and allow you to "see"—when to give you knowledge and insight, and when to show you treasure buried in a field. God wants

2

to manifest Himself at a moment's notice to the one who is ready: *"If any of you wants to serve Me, then follow Me...ready to serve at a moment's notice. The Father will honor and reward anyone who serves Me"* (John 12:26).

Celtic Christians often spoke of "thin places," a place where the curtain between this natural world and the eternal world has been worn thin through prayer. Enoch discovered that thin place and walked out of time into eternity. This "thin place" is where what is real, yet in another dimension, appears through a veil into this world—like the hand that appeared in the Book of Daniel and began writing on the wall. God is ready to download thoughts, answers, solutions, and ideas and to pass them through your thoughts and mind to benefit the world. Are you ready to receive it?

> Individually the disciple and friend of Jesus who has learned to work shoulder to shoulder with his or her Lord stands in this world as a point of contact between heaven and earth, a kind of Jacob's ladder by which the angels of God may ascend from and descend into human life. Thus the disciple stands as an envoy or a receiver by which the kingdom of God is conveyed into every quarter of human affairs.
> —Dallas Willard[2]

We don't often think of "effortlessness" as a characteristic we should cultivate in our lives. Most of us were raised to always try harder and do more in order to maximize our potential. Although my life mission *is* to empower people to maximize their potential, I believe the key is not in maximizing one's *"doing"* as much as one's *"being."*

CHARACTERISTIC 17: EFFORTLESSNESS

When I think of effortlessness, I think of entering God's rest—a major theme throughout the Bible. In Matthew 11:29 (NLT), Jesus said, *"take My yoke upon you. Let Me teach you, because I am humble and gentle at heart, and you will find rest for your souls."*

Living authentically has much to do with living effortlessly—not striving, conniving, manipulating, clamoring to get ahead, etc.

I came across this entry in a classic devotional called *God Calling* that sums up this idea: "Do not be too ready to *do,* just *be.* I said, *'Be ye therefore perfect'* not 'do perfect things.' Try and grasp this. Individual efforts avail nothing. It is only the work of My Spirit that counts." The entry closes with this verse: *"Be still, and know that I am God"* (Ps. 46:10 NLT)—but brings to my mind this verse: *"'Not by might nor by power, but by My Spirit,' says the Lord"* (Zech. 4:6 NIV).

When you rest in God, you are operating from a place of supernatural power, causing everything you do to seem effortless. It may take effort to enter that place (Hebrews 4:11 talks about striving diligently to enter that rest), but it will energize you once you're there:

> *He energizes those who get tired...those who wait upon God get fresh strength. They spread their wings and soar like eagles, they run and don't get tired, they walk and don't lag behind* (Isaiah 40:28-31).

Think how effortlessly the eagle soars on invisible currents—as Job declared to God, *"through Your know-how...the hawk learned to fly, soaring effortlessly on thermal updrafts"* (Job 39:26). Or as David declared, *"God, You floodlight my life; I'm blazing with glory, God's glory! I smash the bands of marauders, I vault the highest fences"* (Ps. 18:28-29).

Where do you need more "know how"—or where in your life are you feeling opposition or boxed in? What does *not* feel effortless?

Try putting effort instead into pursuing God's rest. Practice "being still" and trusting God to lift you up so you soar—no, *vault*—effortlessly over the highest fences. Keep company with God so you learn to live freely and lightly.

> *Are you tired? Worn out? Burned out on religion? Come to Me. Get away with Me and you'll recover your life. I'll show you how to take a real rest. Walk with Me and work with Me—watch how I do it. Learn the unforced rhythms of grace. I won't lay anything heavy or ill-fitting on you. Keep company with Me and you'll learn to live freely and lightly* (Matthew 11:28-30).

Repose is a quality too many undervalue. In the clamor one is irresistibly drawn to the woman who sits gracefully relaxed, who keeps her hands still, talks in a low voice, and listens with responsive eyes and smiles. She creates a spell around her, charming to the ear, the eye and the mind. —Good Housekeeping, November 1947

Day Eighteen

Focusing

It is the set of the sails, not the direction of the wind that determines which way we will go. —Jim Rohn

Focusing your mind is like setting the sails on a sailboat. Marketers are banking on the thoughts and images they plant in your mind causing you to buy their product or service. Spending millions of dollars for 30 seconds of advertising must pay off or they would all go out of business. They know that what you repeatedly see and hear affects what you will do. God also knows that His purposes on Earth depend on the thinking power of His people. That's one of the reasons why He says that you must be transformed by the renewing of your mind (see Rom. 12:2). According to Eugene Peterson, author of *The Message*, your thoughts will determine your destiny. "The way we conceive the future sculpts the present, gives contour and tone to nearly every action and thought through the day. If our sense of future is weak, we live listlessly."[1]

Hiding your thoughts isn't an option; eventually whatever you harbor in the innermost corridors of your thought life will, sooner or later, reveal itself in the outer arena of your present experience. Just as a seed is for a time hidden underground, it will eventually break through the surface, and its true essence will ultimately be revealed—likewise, "[God] *will both bring to light the secret things that are [now hidden] in darkness and disclose and expose the [secret] aims (motives and purposes) of hearts*" (1 Cor. 4:5 AMP).

If you want to change your thought life, you must guard what you allow into your mind and purposefully choose what to focus your thoughts on. This soul fast is a time to eliminate distractions and destructive mindsets by fasting from negative, life-sapping thought patterns and creating new habits of feasting on positive, life-enhancing truths about who God says He is and who you truly are. Winning the battle in your thought-life requires meditating daily on the truths found in Scripture by studying the Word of God.

Memorize God's written Word as Jesus did, so that when satan comes with negative thoughts and lies you can resist him and he will flee. Here's a good one to start with:

> *Whatever is true, whatever is honorable, whatever is right, whatever is pure, whatever is lovely, whatever is of good repute, if there is any excellence and if anything worthy of praise, dwell on these things* (Philippians 4:8 NASB).

God told Joshua, the appointed successor of Moses, that meditating on His Word was the secret to success and prosperity. Joshua was to take what God had already said He wanted to give, the Promised Land, and redistribute it to the world through His people. Joshua could take courage that God would be with him as he went:

> *This book of the law shall not depart from your mouth, but you shall meditate on it day and night, so that you may be careful to do according to all that is written in it; for then you will make your way prosperous, and then you will have success.... Be strong and courageous...for the Lord your God is with you wherever you go* (Joshua 1:8-9 NASB).

Meditating is about focusing your thoughts deeply on the works and words of God and allowing them to direct your life. It comes from a word that means to take the time to mull it over and ruminate on it rather than a casual skimming over the top. It is also about noticing God being present with you. So don't be timid! Focus your thoughts! Take the land! Redistribute to the world the new things God wants to give you!

> If you want to be happy, set a goal that commands your thoughts, liberates your energy, and inspires your hopes. —Andrew Carnegie

This week we have been talking about the nature of the soul. Your soul is the divine, eternal essence of you. An uncluttered, healed, and whole soul represents your true, authentic self. Learning to living authentically is what *The 40 Day Soul Fast* is all about.

CHARACTERISTIC 18: AUTHENTICITY

So what is authenticity?

Authenticity simply means being true to who you are—aligning your every thought and action with who and what you were created to be and do. Nothing or nobody should define you—it is up to you to understand who you are and live according to that truth. As Harvey S. Firestone once said, "Accept no one's definition of your life, but define yourself."

I believe this is what it means to guard you soul. Joshua 23:11 commands that you *"vigilantly guard your souls."* Guard your soul from falsehood—from living a façade that leads to deception and living inauthentically. It's up to you to maintain the integrity of your own soul.

You alone are responsible to "know thyself" as Socrates advised, and "to your own self be true" as Shakespeare so famously said. People have climbed the tallest mountains, crossed uncharted waters, navigated rivers, explored the great frontier of outer space, but the last of our greatest challenges still awaits us—the final frontier—the inner space of our spirits and the hidden innate potential of our own souls. Only you can chart that journey for yourself and make that discovery known. You must become the "Christopher Columbus" of your own life.

"You are your greatest asset. Put your time, effort, and money into training, grooming, and encouraging your greatest asset," said Tom Hopkins. Be yourself. Never be tempted to become an imitator of another. No one is better than you at being you. We all have something unique to give. Do not compare yourself with anyone else. Dare to maintain your uniqueness and divine originality. Set the standard, be an example, raise the bar—when you do, you give others permission to do the same. Thoreau said, "If a man does not keep pace with his companions, perhaps it is because he hears a different drummer. Let him step to the music which he hears, however measured or far away." Take the lead in letting others step to the music they hear by dancing to your own.

Become your own choreographer and perfect your moves, then seek out opportunities to show them off. "Ability is nothing without opportunity," said Napoleon Bonaparte. Accept no limits, explore every opportunity, and lift every lid. Discover that thing that turns you on and do it with passion. Be bold with it. Johan Wolfgang Von Goethe said, "Boldness has genius and power in it." King Solomon said, *"A man's gift makes room for him, and brings him before great men"* (Prov. 18:16 NKJV). Stir up the gift within you and make room! "Never be bullied into silence or beaten into existing as a non-entity," said the great industrialist, Harvey S. Firestone, "Accept no one's definition of your life, but maintain your God given right to define or redefine yourself according to your understanding of who God made you to be." John F. Kennedy said, "Let us resolve to be masters, not the victims, of our history, controlling our own destiny."

Your faith, love, patience, peace, and understanding—which are by-products of living authentically—will always be tested. It is this "proving" that refines and matures us. It is what helps us get at the true essence and core of who we are in Christ. You must continually *"prove the authenticity of your love," "test what is authentically right,"* and be stirred and *"reminded of your authentic faith"* (2 Cor. 8:8 CEB; John 7:24; 2 Tim. 1:5 CEB). When all is said and done, you will know what about you *"was authentic and proved sure"* (Heb. 2:2 AMP).

Dare to live authentically. *"Examine yourselves to see if your faith is genuine. Test yourselves"* (2 Cor. 13:5 NLT).

- If God were to drop a plumb line into the building you've created of your life, how aligned would it be with His original blueprint for you? (See Amos 7:7-8.)

- How can you realign your life so that it reflects the authentic you God had in mind?

Anyone who intends to come with Me has to let Me lead. You're not in the driver's seat; I am. Don't run from suffering; embrace it. Follow Me and I'll show you how. Self-help is no help at all. Self-sacrifice is the way, My way, to saving yourself, your true self. What good would it do to get everything you want and lose you, the real you? What could you ever trade your soul for? (Mark 8:34)

That inner voice has both gentleness and clarity. So to get to authenticity, you really keep going down to the bone, to the honesty, and the inevitability of something. —Meredith Monk

Day Nineteen

Envisioning

> The greatest achievement was at first and for a time a dream. The oak sleeps in the acorn, the bird waits in the egg, and in the highest vision of the soul a waking angel stirs. Dreams are the seedlings of realities. —James Allen

Thought is not limited to reality. You can envision something that does not currently exist in that present form; you can see yourself doing something you can't currently do. That is a loose definition of *creativity*: "to make or bring into existence something new; to invest a thing with a new form." Creativity requires a degree of faith. In fact, faith is simply a matter of first seeing things differently in your mind, and then being convinced of a future potential outcome that does not yet exist.

In Luke 17:5 (NLT), Jesus was asked by His disciples, *"Show us how to increase our faith."* His curious answer was the story of a servant who had completed the work he was told to do. Then Jesus asked, "Does the servant get special thanks for doing what was expected of him?"

Why did Jesus offer this as an illustration of how to increase your faith?

Jesus meant that if you want more out of life, if you want the capacity to believe God for more, you must be prepared to do more than your duty. Dallas Willard says that Jesus is often seen more as a sheepdog than a Shepherd—barking out orders and telling people what to do. Duty and obedience are part of how God operates, but He wants so much more for you than that:

> *Live creatively, friends.... Make a careful exploration of who you are and the work you have been given, and then sink yourself into that. Don't be impressed with yourself. Don't compare yourself with others. Each of you must take responsibility for doing the creative best you can with your own life* (Galatians 6:1,4-5).

If you plan to change your future, don't set your mind on things or people or circumstances that are smaller than what you desire to see manifested in that future. Paul said we are to live in the wide-open spaces of God's grace and glory (see Rom. 5:2). Replace small thinking with a clear vision of what that bigger picture looks like, down to blueprint-like details you can almost touch, taste, smell, hear, and see. That's what God did with Abraham in Genesis 13, telling him to look at the territory he was giving him. He had Abraham walk the land in every direction, visualizing his legacy as he ran sand through his fingers and heard God saying, "For every grain of sand, you will have a descendent." God was planting a vision in Abraham's mind of his destiny.

Your ability to harness your imagination determines whether life's opportunities will shrink or expand. Albert Einstein, a scientific genius at imagining unseen opportunities said, "I am enough of an artist to draw freely upon my imagination. Imagination is more than knowledge. Knowledge is limited. Imagination encircles the world."

Oswald Chambers proclaimed that imagination was the greatest gift of God next to salvation because it allows you to see yourself in the throne room of God. That's living large!

Purpose to think inspired thoughts—thoughts from God Himself as He expresses His will through your mind:

Because we know that this extraordinary day is just ahead, we pray for you all the time—pray that our God will make you fit for what He's called you to be, pray that He'll fill your good ideas and acts of faith with His own energy so that it all amounts to something (2 Thessalonians 1:11).

Ask God to enlarge your capacity to think, to be able to take the limits off—to give you the ability to see in your mind the seed of massive potential He has planted in your heart.

Your vision will become clear only when you look into your heart. Who looks outside, dreams. Who looks inside, awakens. —Carl Jung

Basically, the life and reality you are experiencing are a reflection of the thoughts you are thinking. This is why you are told in Psalm to *"guard your heart above all else, for it determines the course of your life"* (Prov. 4:23 NLT). Ultimately, the power of our thoughts translates into our ability to focus. It's focused thought that wields the greatest power.

CHARACTERISTIC 19: FOCUS

The number one thing that keeps people from realizing their goals, maximizing their potential, and fulfilling their purpose is focus. Wherever you place your focus, the rest of your mind, talents, abilities, and emotions will follow.

Let me give you an example from the world of racecar driving. As I understand it, when new drivers are learning how to race, one of the very first things they are taught is what to focus on when they go into a spin. If they try to avoid hitting the wall, they usually wind up hitting it. Why? Because avoiding the wall means that they must focus on the wall. So they are taught instead to focus on where it is they want to go—fix their sight on a destination outside of the spin and away from the wall. If drivers fix their focus on the road ahead, that is where they are more likely to find themselves.

Let me give you another example. When I was a young girl, I studied ballet. When pirouetting, I was trained to "spot" or focus on a particular place or spot where we desired to end our spin. A pirouette is as a 360-degree spin, for non-ballet enthusiasts. In both cases, focus is the key to success. Sometimes our lives can spin out of control like a racecar driver, or we can spin "in control" like a ballerina. Focus is the key to getting in and out of life's spins with success and precision.

Here's the rule I want you to remember: People who focus on what they want get exactly what they want; people who focus on what they don't want, get exactly what they don't want. If you focus on problems, hurdles, walls, and obstacles, you will go through life with problems, hurdles, walls, and obstacles. It's not what's happening to you now, or what has happened to you in the past, that determines who you become. Rather, it is your focus on it. It is the meaning and significance that you give to every occurrence that determines its influence upon your life.

Your focus will determine your future. This is why Paul talked so much about focusing his mind on the task set before him. There is uncommon, unstoppable power in setting your mind on Christ, on things above, and on the high calling set before you. As Paul stated in his letter to the Philippians:

I've got my eye on the goal, where God is beckoning us onward…I'm off and running, and I'm not turning back. So let's keep focused on that goal, those of us who want everything God has for us. If any of you have something else in mind, something less than total commitment, God will clear your blurred vision—you'll see it yet! Now that we're on the right track, let's stay on it (Philippians 3:14-16).

Whatever you focus on today, you give that thing permission to exist tomorrow. Focus on your dreams, future, goals, and vision. Focus on where you want to be, not where you came from. Focus on what you expect to acquire and what you wish to do, not on what you do not have and what you have not done. Focus on your healing and not your sickness. Focus on your deliverance and not your detrimental situations. Focus on what remains and not what you have lost. Focus on wearing those size 7 skinny jeans and not on how much weight you have gained. Dream about how different your life can be, then wake up and focus on making it happen so that you can live the life of your dreams. Think about it only enough to formulate a plan and then put feet to that plan by focusing on making it happen. Contemplate it long enough so that your faith becomes the driving force of your focus. Talk about it long enough so that you motivate yourself to act.

Focus makes your faith unshakable. Focus eliminates distractions. Focus is quintessential to discipline, which is always the precursor to success and prosperity. If you do not want to see something in your future, do not focus on it today. Train your mind to focus on the positive, and you will always have positive outcomes.

Paul wrote the Corinthians, *"It was God who kept us focused on Him, uncompromised"* (2 Cor. 1:12). And this is what David prayed:

> *O God, God of our fathers Abraham, Isaac, and Israel, keep this generous spirit alive forever in these people always, keep their hearts set firmly in You. And give my son...an uncluttered and focused heart* (1 Chronicles 29:18).

Jesus knew lack of focus was at the core of the "evil generation" He faced: *"What a generation! No sense of God! No focus to your lives!"* (Matt. 17:17). And so Paul prayed this on behalf of Christ's followers:

> *I ask—ask the God of our Master, Jesus Christ, the God of glory—to make you intelligent and discerning in knowing Him personally, your eyes focused and clear, so that you can see exactly what it is He is calling you to do* (Ephesians 1:16).

- What is God calling you to do? Focus on your calling, not your circumstances.

- What is it you want more of? If you want more of God and His power working in your life, focus on God and His power!

I encourage you with Philippians 4:7-8:

> *And the peace of God, which surpasses all comprehension, will guard your hearts and your minds in Christ Jesus. Finally, brethren, whatever is true, whatever is honorable, whatever is right, whatever is pure, whatever is lovely, whatever is of good repute, if there is any excellence and if*

anything worthy of praise, dwell on these things (Philippians 4:7-8 NASB).

Focus on what you want, not what you don't want! Do not allow anything or anyone to alter your focus.

Our thoughts create our reality—where we put our focus is the direction we tend to go. —Peter McWilliams

Keep your eyes straight ahead; ignore all sideshow distractions. Watch your step, and the road will stretch out smooth before you. Look neither right nor left; leave evil in the dust (Proverbs 4:24-27).

Day Twenty

Conquering

It is the image of God reflected in you that so enrages hell; it is this at which the demons hurl their mightiest weapons. —William Gurnall

Don't be naïve. You have an enemy who is determined to steal your destiny, kill your heart, and destroy everything you care about. He wants to convince you that you're not worthy of God's love and that you are inadequate of achieving something great. He doesn't have to eliminate you, but merely control your thoughts. It would be easy to recognize and resist him and his cohorts if they came to you and told you to overtly sin—rob a bank or murder your neighbor. But his favorite ploy is to disguise himself as truth, an angel of light, and invade your thoughts with deceit that is just a little off-center. Then a compounding factor, much like the rate of interest, takes over. The first thought gets built upon by another thought; a lie believed gets added to another lie; until finally that single erroneous thought becomes a major controlling pattern in your life. That is what the Scripture calls a stronghold, a place of imprisonment:

> So, it becomes the devil's business to keep the Christian's spirit imprisoned. He knows that the believing and justified Christian has been raised up out of the grave of his sins and trespasses. From that point on, Satan works that much harder to keep us bound and gagged, actually imprisoned in our own grave clothes. He knows that if we continue in this kind of

bondage...we are not much better off than when we were spiritually dead. —A.W. Tozer

We are told in Ephesians that the battles we find ourselves in are not with other humans, but with unseen beings that are quite real and dwell outside our 3D world:

For we wrestle not against flesh and blood, but against principalities, against powers, against the rulers of the darkness of this world, against spiritual wickedness in high places (Ephesians 6:12 KJV).

It's easy to ignore something or someone you can't see. Many Christians today aren't really sure whether they believe such beings even exist. That's exactly what satan wants. Author and scientist Gary Sutliff finds that belief surprising since "secular scientists, after a legacy of denial of anything beyond what can be seen and tested, are now postulating on parallel universes and other possible realms."[1] Many examples throughout the Old and New Testament speak clearly about the reality of these cross-dimensional encounters and the consequences of not taking authority over such entities. You can't afford to be complacent. Your life depends upon you being vigilant and sober-minded:

Therefore gird up the loins of your mind, be sober, and rest your hope fully upon the grace that is to be brought to you at the revelation of Jesus Christ (1 Peter 1:13 NKJV).

God has already equipped you with the weapons necessary to win—conquering your thought life and the associated false reasoning and logic:

For though we walk in the flesh, we do not war according to the flesh, for the weapons of our warfare are not

of the flesh, but divinely powerful for the destruction of fortresses. We are destroying speculations and every lofty thing raised up against the knowledge of God, and we are taking every thought captive to the obedience of Christ (2 Corinthians 10:3-5 NASB).

Taking control of your thoughts will cause you to gain control of your life. You have inherited the Kingdom and have been given dominion over all your adversaries—and you must think like it! You must command your raging thoughts like Jesus commanded the sea—be still! Put good things in your mind:

Whatever things are true, whatever things are noble, whatever things are just, whatever things are pure, whatever things are lovely, whatever things are of good report, if there is any virtue and if there is anything praiseworthy—meditate on these things...and the God of peace will be with you (Philippians 4:8-9 NKJV).

Dallas Willard says that thoughts and images are the primary focus of satan's efforts to defeat God's purposes and that a life of worship is the single most powerful force in completing and sustaining restoration of your soul. Bless the Lord, O my soul!

Nothing is orderly till man takes hold of it. Everything in creation lies around loose. —Henry Ward Beecher

Yesterday we talked about the power of focus. Sometimes it is a challenge to not only *set* our focus on what we should, but to *keep* our focus once we do. One of the tools—or characteristics—that will help you set and keep your focus is learning to order your thoughts.

CHARACTERISTIC 20: ORDER

We have already talked about the need *to "take every thought captive to make it obedient to Christ"* (2 Cor. 10:5 NIV). But more than ordering our thoughts, we must learn to "order our days."

A cluttered environment is a sign of a cluttered, confused soul. De-clutter your environment so that you can de-clutter your life. Bring order to your closet, drawers, garage, car, finances, and relationships. When you bring order into your life, you will help to dissolve stress and tension to awaken creativity. Order gives you clarity of thought and greater control over your time. Order brings freshness to your environment and vitality to your soul. Order allows you to plan your activities according to specific time frames. Losing time because of a lack of order will cost you dearly in the future. Stick to a plan. Bring order to your health by going to bed at a regular hour and eating on schedule.

Nothing will help you to keep order in your mind more than establishing order in your daily life. I'm talking about making the most of your time every day and eliminating "time wasters"—if your day is cluttered or full of toxic activities, so will be your mind! Junk time is as bad as junk food! Take account of the empty time calories that make up the daily sustenance of your life in the form of television watching, Internet surfing, magazine perusing, or even gossiping with coworkers. As Paul told the Ephesians, *"Don't live carelessly, unthinkingly"* (Eph. 5:17); and *"make every minute count"* (Eph. 5:16 CEV).

In other words, plan your work and work your plan. Establish order in your life. Proverbs advises, *"Consider well the path of your feet, and let all your ways be established and ordered aright"* (Prov. 4:26 AMP). God is a God of order. Study out how God does whatever He does according to a certain order. Hebrews 9 and 10 talk about the "old order" and the "new order" when referring to the Old and New Testaments. Hebrews 7 talks about a change in the order of priesthood from that of Levi and Aaron to Melchizedek. In Christ, you and I represent that new order.

"Righteousness" is defined as *"conformity with God's will and order"* (Isa. 54:14 AMP). David, the most righteous king of all, prayed to the Lord: *"teach us to number our days, that we may gain a heart of wisdom"* (Ps. 90:12 NIV). In other words, he prayed that God would show him how to order his time so that he might become wise.

- As you sit quietly in the presence of God, take an account of how you spend or allocate each hour of each day, just like you keep an account of how you spend money or allocate calories.

- How can you "reorder" your day to help you better order your thoughts?

- How does the order, or lack of order, in your home, office, car, or garage affect the order, or lack of order, in your soul? Is there room for more order? How will you bring that to pass? When?

As the father of modern management theory, Peter Drucker, so famously said, "Until we can manage time, we can manage nothing else."

The bad news is time flies. The good news is you're the pilot. —Michael Altshuler

Look carefully then how you walk! Live purposefully and worthily and accurately, not as the unwise and witless, but as wise (sensible, intelligent people), Making the very most of the time [buying up each opportunity], because the days are evil. Therefore do not be vague and thoughtless and foolish, but understanding and firmly grasping what the will of the Lord is (Ephesians 5:15-17 AMP).

This is the beginning of a new day. God has given me this day to use as I will. I can waste it or use it for good. What I do today is important, because I am exchanging a day of my life for it. When tomorrow comes, this day will be gone forever, leaving in its place something that I have traded for it. I want it to be gain, not loss; good not evil; success not failure; in order that I shall not regret the price I paid for it. —Author Unknown

Week Five

The Importance of Identity: Becoming a Master by Mastering Your Mind

Day Twenty-one

Embracing

*Ask me whether what I have done is **my** life.*
—William Stafford

Who are you really? Have you ever asked yourself that question in earnest? Most of us are so focused on what we do day-to-day—often struggling to meet the expectations of others—that we don't stop to ask who we are created to be. I am convinced that if we focus more on our character—beginning with the 40 characteristics I've outlined here—rather than our career or the company we keep—we would be living more meaningful and impactful lives. We would be able to tap into the unique strengths and creative potential with which we have each been endowed. We would move beyond the cookie-cutter lives that so many have found to be shallow and unfulfilling.

Apart from what you do, the roles you play, the family you grew up in—who *are* you?

This week we will begin talking about what is at the very heart of *The 40 Day Soul Fast*—getting in touch with the real you. For those of us living in a western culture, this can seem elusive. Our identity is largely defined by what we do. When you are asked to introduce yourself, you might go beyond what you do for a living to talk about where you are from, where you went to school, your family, the roles you play in various relationships—whether you're a spouse, parent, or other type of caregiver—or involved in a church or other organization, or volunteer in the community. You may even "name drop" to elevate your status in the conversation. Wholeness and meaning in life, however, do not result from the activities you're involved in, the people you know, or even the titles you hold, although sometimes it seems like it.

For others, answering questions about themselves is extremely awkward. Some fear being judged or criticized, or that they will be discovered as an imposter due to negative labels and images from the past. Over time, we find we become less and less authentic with others, as well as ourselves. Battling the forces that want to diminish you and hold you down can feel overwhelming. Often it seems easier to allow the people around you to dictate who you are and slip into a life of mediocrity and dullness. Raymond Hull offers this warning: "He who trims himself to suit everyone will soon whittle himself away."

Rather than risking the doubts and disappointments from controlling people in your life, you settle into a good, moral existence. "Good enough" becomes your mantra. The burning desires God put in your being when He created you ever so slowly grow cold. You begin sleepwalking through life, living vicariously through your children, the lives of people in books or shows on television, or famous people in society or sports. As one author puts it, your life becomes deathly safe.

Wake up! It's time to embrace your authentic life, the life God uniquely designed for you! Ephesians 5:14 is a personal directive from God to you: *"Wake up from your sleep, climb out of your coffins; Christ will show you the light!"* Fan into flame the tiny embers of passion you may not even be aware are still there.

So who do *you* say you are?

It's impossible to live for very long in opposition to the way you see yourself—positively or negatively. Sooner or later, the thoughts and images in your mind will manifest themselves in how you live. If you are to live more authentically, you must embrace the importance of your identity. You are your Heavenly Father's child—literally. You have His DNA imprinted in your spirit, encoded in your heart. You have been made a partaker of His divine nature *"as His divine power has given to us all things that pertain to life and godliness"* (2 Pet. 1:3 NKJV). Grab hold of this truth. Believe it is so. Wrap your mind around what it means in regards to how you live. Set your mind on hearing from your heart.

Understanding your identity in Christ and how you are to reflect that are absolutely essential to your success at living an authentic life. Since you were created in His image, the more you know about Him, the more you will learn about yourself and how to live in the victory and abundance He has for you. *"Watch what God does,"* as it says in Ephesians 5:1, *"and then you do it."* This week will talk about four key components of better understanding and walking in your true identity—agreeing, capitalizing, belonging, and becoming.

> The value of identity, of course, is that so often with it comes purpose. —Richard R. Grant

This week we are addressing the characteristics of an authentic person having to do with the importance of identity. Most recently, we have talked about the characteristics of "focus" and "order"—focusing our thoughts by ordering our day. Some days this seems to come easier than others. It's not always easy to master your time and your mind in the most effective manner. This is where faith comes in.

CHARACTERISTIC 21: FAITH

An unknown author shared a story about a young lady who was driving along with her father. They came upon a storm, and the young lady asked her father, "What should I do?"

He said, "Keep driving."

Cars began pulling over to the side of the road as the storm grew worse. "What should I do?" the young lady asked.

"Keep driving," her father replied.

On up a few feet, she noticed that eighteen-wheelers were also pulling over. She told her dad, "I must pull over, I can barely see ahead. It is terrible, and everyone is pulling over!"

Her father told her, "Don't give up, just keep driving!" As the storm intensified, she never stopped driving, and soon she could see a little more clearly. After a couple of miles she was again on dry land, and the sun came out. Her father said, "Now you can pull over and get out."

She asked, "But why now?"

He said, "Because now that you are through the storm, you can get out and see the view—you can look back and see all the people who gave up and are still mired in the storm."

This story touched me because we all have those times when we want to quit, but as the Bible says, "The race is not given to the swift or to the strong," but to the person who endures to the end (see Eccles 9:10-12). Your faith will empower you to endure. Never give up, because God will never give up on you. Sometimes, when all else fails, you just need to follow God's instructions and believe. He is your heavenly Father, and *"with God all things are possible...to him who believes"* (Matt. 19:26; Mark 9:23 NKJV).

There is nothing on this Earth that compares with the power of belief. It is belief that changes circumstances, alters destinies, and fuels miracles. Jesus said, *"If you have faith and don't doubt, you can do things like this and much more.... You can pray for anything, and if you have faith, you will receive it"* (Matt. 21:21-22 NLT); *"when you pray, believe that you receive"* (Mark 11:24); *"don't be afraid; just believe"* (Mark 5:36; Luke 8:50 NIV).

Believing faith will keep you rooted and grounded in authenticity. Pinpoint those things you struggle with on a day-to-day basis that keep you from making the most of your time or distract you in the arena of your mind. Exercise your faith by believing God will provide what you need to overcome any obstacles—declare what you need and confess victory over the hindrances keeping your authentic self from shining through. It is by faith you preserve your soul. The writer of Hebrews wrote: *"We are of those who believe and by faith preserve the soul"* (Heb. 10:39 AMP). Take charge of your day, your thoughts—and your soul—by faith.

If you want to live authentically—live true to your divine self as Christ did when He was alive on the Earth—then stir up your faith every moment of every day. *"For if we are faithful to the end, trusting God just as firmly as when we first believed, we will share in all that belongs to Christ"* (Heb. 3:14 NLT).

I've grown certain that the root of all fear is that we've been forced to deny who we are. —Frances Moore Lappe

Through Him we received both the generous gift of His life and the urgent task of passing it on to others.... You are who you are through this gift and call of Jesus Christ! (Romans 1:2)

Day Twenty-two

Agreeing

> One of the greatest dangers in the spiritual life is
> self-rejection.... To grow beyond self-rejection we
> must have the courage to listen to the voice calling
> us God's beloved sons and daughters, and the
> determination always to live our lives according to
> this truth. —Henri Nouwen[1]

Poor self-image is like a harness of slavery on your soul.
Christ came to set you free from the bondage of shame,
guilt, self-doubt, fear, and unworthiness. *"It is for freedom that Christ has set us free"* (Gal. 5:1a NIV). Paul wrote the
Galatians instructing them to *"Stand firm, then, and do not let
yourselves be burdened again by a yoke of slavery"* (Gal. 5:1b NIV).
Never again doubt that you are worthy, gifted, and highly
valued. Self-rejection is the greatest enemy of your spiritual
life because, as Brennan Manning states, "It contradicts the
whole idea of being beloved by God."[2] That's who you are—
the beloved of Christ.

In the greatest love song ever written, the Song of Solomon, the lover prophetically depicted is Jesus Himself, who is
calling you *"His beloved,"* saying that He wants to see *your* face,
He wants to hear *your* voice, and He wants to run with *you* on
the mountaintops! God wants you to stop hiding and come
openly and boldly to Him. No more masks, no more pretend-
ing, no more fear. It's the authentic you He lovingly invites
into the best future you can imagine!

Authenticity is based on living in agreement with what God says about you. It's about being grateful for your past, believing that "adversity introduces you to yourself." You can thank God in advance for your future because you know that He is always working all things out for your good (see Rom. 8:28). Living authentically is about throwing open the barred doors of your heart and shouting, "Yes!" As Dag Hammarskjold, former UN Secretary General, famously stated, "For all that has been—Thanks! For all that shall be—Yes!"

You may be saying to yourself that this is all well and good for those whose lives are spotless and not subject to shortcomings and weaknesses, however, living authentically is not about gaining the approval of people, but of God who loves you just as you are. Trying to cover up the pain from your past—and the corresponding feelings that get buried in your soul as a result—will send you searching for a substitute evidence of your value. Basking in the applause of others for an amazing achievement provides only temporary relief, the effect of which quickly wears off, and soon you're looking for a new feat and another fix. Who would you be if all that were stripped away?

Your soul has both limits and potentials that create a tension within which you must learn to live with. God doesn't expect flawlessness. As Parker Palmer put it, "What a long time it can take to become the person one has always been!" Your authentic self unfolds like a Polaroid picture—a little at a time as you replace the negative images with powerful images of God's amazing love for you, regardless of your perceived imperfections.

Brain researcher Dr. Caroline Leaf has seen the evidence of negative thinking, including unforgiveness, on the brain. She writes that 87 to 95 percent of the illnesses that plague people today are a direct result of their thought life. Fear alone triggers more than 1,400 known physical and chemical responses and activates more than thirty different hormones. But where God's love is, there is no fear—it is cast out!

You can't will away much of your life, but you can change how you think about it. Ask God to free you of the yokes of slavery in your mind. Start seeing yourself as God sees you—beautiful! Not because of what you've done, but because of who you are—His beloved. In the Song of Solomon, Jesus says that *you* have *"ravished"* His heart! Let that sink deep into your soul today.

> What would I find in my own heart if the noise of the world were silenced? Who would I be? Who will I be, when loss or crisis or the depredations of time take away the trappings of success, of self-importance, even personality itself? —Kathleen Norris[3]

Your thought life is critical to the health of your soul. And there's nothing more critical to the health of your thought life than your attitude! You've heard it said that attitude determines altitude. Today, I want to propose that it's an attitude of gratitude that determines the degree to which you will be able to live true to your authentic self.

CHARACTERISTIC 22: GRATITUDE

How grateful are you for who God created you to be? Gratitude for your unique combination of strengths, abilities, and special gifts will enable you to stay true to your calling. What unique role has God created you to fulfill? What has God set you apart to do that only you—being you—can do? Be grateful for where God has placed you, what He has you doing, when He has you doing it, and who—as in the unique expression of His own image—He is causing you to become. *"Serve the Lord your God with joyfulness of [mind and] heart [in gratitude] for the abundance of all [with which He had blessed you]"* (Deut. 28:47 AMP). Just as you can never "out-bless" God, you can never thank Him enough either.

- What five strengths, abilities, or talents about yourself are you grateful for?

- List five opportunities or outcomes that you have not yet experienced that you can preemptively be grateful for? (Now you are building faith!)

- Who are the people in your life you are especially grateful for? What can you do to make this known to them—and when?

- How much time do you invest praising and thanking God, focusing on all the good gifts and blessings He has bestowed—versus the time you spend grumbling and complaining, focusing on all that is wrong and not what you imagine it should be?

Look for opportunities to be grateful and to show gratitude! *"Stay alert, with your eyes wide open in gratitude"* (Col. 4:2).

The unthankful heart discovers no mercies; but let the thankful heart sweep through the day and, as the magnet finds the iron, so it will find, in every hour, some heavenly blessings! —Henry Ward Beecher

He is a wise man who does not grieve for the things which he has not, but rejoices for those which he has. —Epictetus

Agreeing

I thank Christ Jesus our Lord, who has given me strength to do His work. He considered me trustworthy and appointed me to serve Him (1 Timothy 1:12 NLT).

Day Twenty-three

Capitalizing

The rubber meets the road when a potential yes means saying a thousand no's to a legion of legitimate choices. We are meant to say our core "yes" to our most central, well-contoured passion that draws forth and reveals God's beauty. —Dan Allendar[1]

Knowledge about why you do what you do—as well as what you are capable of—will give you the ability to minimize your weaknesses while capitalizing on your strengths. This is vital to the health of your soul and essential to your empowerment. There are a myriad of personality assessments and "spiritual gifts" testing tools that can give you insight into your hidden potential, directing you toward your unique purpose. Gallup produced one such tool, the Clifton StrengthsFinder, after 30 years of research on human potential. In over two million interviews, they found the evidence overwhelming: "You will be most successful in whatever you do by building your life around your greatest natural abilities rather than your weaknesses."[2] They go on to explain to the person taking the test:

Like everyone, you've been blessed by God with a deep reservoir of untapped potential. That potential is your talent, waiting to be discovered and put to use in your life. It's time for you to unleash the power of that potential and begin to discover your unique talents.[3]

Do all you can to understand how God has made you. Ephesians 2:10 states you are *"His workmanship, created in Christ Jesus for good works, which God prepared beforehand that* [you] *should walk in them"* (NKJV). However, your heart, mind, soul, and body were never intended to operate outside a relationship with God and His power. That means that it is never *only* about your strengths and talents, but it is those attributes in conjunction with the Spirit of God.

Most people have at least a cursory knowledge of the story of David and Goliath found in First Samuel 17. They read it as a story about a young boy who takes his well-honed shepherding skills and stands up to a belligerent giant threatening to destroy God's people. You probably know that David won the battle with a slingshot and a single stone, striking Goliath in the forehead. David said, as he went out with great, heroic courage:

> *I come at you in the name of God-of-the-Angel-Armies... The whole earth will know that there's an extraordinary God in Israel. And everyone gathered here will learn that God doesn't save by means of sword or spear. The battle belongs to God—He's handing you to us on a platter* (1 Samuel 17:45-47).

It's what comes after this passage that is especially worthy of remembering. When King Saul saw David the shepherd boy going out to fight with an enemy much more powerful than he was, Saul asked the commander of his army, "Who is this kid?" Abner's reply was priceless: *"For the life of me, O King, I don't know"* (1 Sam. 17:55). David understood that it wasn't about his great talents, but about God joining with him to accomplish God's purposes in a way that God would get the glory.

To be a weapon in the hand of God can be a frightening thing. Rather than embrace your destiny you may deny your potential. What a loss to the world! Be strong and courageous! The battle belongs to God! It is your destiny!

> Our deepest fear is not that we are inadequate. Our deepest fear is that we are powerful beyond measure. It is our light, not our darkness, that most frightens us. We ask ourselves, "Who am I to be brilliant, gorgeous, talented, and fabulous?" Actually, who are you not to be? You are a child of God. Your playing small doesn't serve the world. —Marianne Williamson

Today I want to talk about destiny as it relates to living authentically. Your divine self has a divine destiny! Over and over in the Bible we read how God orchestrates our destinies—how He has called and anointed all who would *"just believe"* (Mark 5:36 NIV) to step forward and *"be strong and courageous"* (Josh. 1:6 NIV) in taking possession of all He has prepared for them.

CHARACTERISTIC 23: DESTINY

Anthony Robbins is quoted as saying, "More than anything else, I believe it's our decisions, not the conditions of our lives, that determine our destiny. It is in your moments of decision that your destiny is shaped."

The earth is the domain of decisions. It is where human beings have the right to choose good or evil, blessing or cursing, success or failure, life or death. Every morning you awaken to unlimited possibilities. The moment you make a decision, a myriad of possibilities collapse and life brings to you your reality in the form of an experience. You must then decide how you will respond to your reality. Failure to make a decision is a decision to fail.

Your destiny is decision-oriented. If you do not like where you are, make a decision to be somewhere else. If you do not like what you have, make a decision to have something else. If you do not like the way your life is, make a decision to live the life you've always dreamed of. You are always only one decision away from living the life of your dreams.

When you make haphazard decisions, you play Russian roulette with your future at point blank range. Never make a permanent decision based on temporary conditions. Be intentional as you deliberate. Consult God about every decision you make. Do not lean on your own understanding. God has already chosen a path that leads you to abundance and eternal life. According to John 10:10, Christ came so that you would have an abundant life. The first decision you should make, therefore, is to invite Him into your heart to be your Savior. The next is to allow Him to be Lord over your life. He will remove the curse, lift the burdens, and usher you into a world filled with blessings. Choose life and not death. Choose to be blessed and not cursed. The choice is yours.

All of the great patriarchs of the Old Testament, though called and anointed, also had to make a choice—they had to choose to believe. We have already talked about how Abraham, Joseph, Moses, Joshua, and David were all "destiny-minded"—how they saw past their situations and limitations and were able to see instead all that was possible with God. They set their course by choosing to believe what they heard God say about their potential.

To live true to your authentic self, you must continually choose to focus on your prospective future as opposed to your current position. Your present self is but the bud of the full flower you are destined to become—but it's up to you to decide whether or not you will bloom.

Take time to reflect on who it is you are becoming and where you are longing to go. Look up from your daily grindstone on occasion. As you tread along day by day, glance up from your stony path once in a while to see the greater landscape—look into the distance upon the hills "from where your help comes from" (see Ps. 121:1 NIV).

- What do you hear God saying about who He has called you to be?

- Paint a picture in your mind of your greatest possible future—write down what you see.

Time in the Word and in prayer will take you up higher, where you can get a wider, more scenic view. Press into God. Put on the mind of Christ. Become "possibility-minded."

Do not be like the woman who *"did not consider her destiny* [and] *therefore her collapse was awesome"* (Lam. 1:9 NKJV). Instead, pursue God's leading through prayer as David did: *"You guide me with Your counsel, leading me to a glorious destiny"* (Ps. 73:24 NLT).

Destiny is no matter of chance. It is a matter of choice. It is not a thing to be waited for, it is a thing to be achieved. —William Jennings Bryan

Our destiny changes with our thought; we shall become what we wish to become, do what we wish to do, when our habitual thought corresponds with our desire. —Orison Swett Marden

I'll show up and take care of you as I promised and bring you back home. I know what I'm doing. I have it all planned out—plans to take care of you, not abandon you, plans to give you the future you hope for (Jeremiah 29:11).

Day Twenty-four

Belonging

> Satan tempts us to be entirely diverse with no unity or entirely a unity with no diversity. If he can succeed he eliminates babies, new life, growth, change, discovery, wonder, the birthing of destinies. —Pastor Peter Hiett[1]

Have you ever been in the midst of a crowd or social gathering and felt lonely? Loneliness is one of our greatest fears and most intense emotional pains. The greatest need of the human heart is the need to belong—the need for connection. We are engineered for connectedness. This is why we are called to be *"one in Christ"* (see Gal. 3:28; Eph. 2:11). "One body"—no divisions, no gender divides, no positional hierarchies—we are all one.

A deceptive tactic of the enemy of our soul is to cause us to believe we are separate. That we are alone—unwanted, unworthy, unloved. Nothing is farther from the truth. Yet all of us struggle with feelings of separateness. Nobody likes to be alone for an extended period of time. But still we can feel lonely even when surrounded by friends, family, and people who love us. Coping with feelings of aloneness can be extremely challenging, particularly for people with low self-esteem—these people are particularly vulnerable to feeling disconnected and isolated. But Jesus came to let every person know they are loved, valued, and never, ever alone.

Just before His crucifixion, Jesus prayed to His Father that people would know His love for them. He prayed that people would live in one accord, united together in that love, as a family of brothers and sisters—all so the world would see and believe that God loves people and know that Jesus came to make a way for everyone to be adopted into God's loving family (see John 17). What an amazing goal—to bring all of humanity together under one roof, that everyone everywhere would be part of one big family! It seems so simple, yet as we've discovered since Jesus ascended to the right hand of the Father, it is not so easily played out. From a human point of view, such thinking would require that God make everyone alike. We see a family and observe the similarities—it seems strange if a person from the same family looks or acts too differently from the other members of the family. You've heard it said, "The apple never falls far from the tree." After all, don't we all need to be alike in order to agree?

That, of course, is exactly the opposite of what God had in mind. Sameness isn't a Kingdom principle, but connectedness is. We do not all have to be the same to be connected. Look at the human body. Are we all an eye, or a nose, or a toe?

The problem is—or maybe it's the solution—that you were created with a deep need to be completed through connection and belonging; to live a common life with others and to act on their behalf. This is what gives our lives meaning. It's why crawling into a cave of independent thinking and living won't work. You were created to love and be loved.

> *Through Him we received both the generous gift of His life and the urgent task of passing it on to others who receive it by entering into obedient trust in Jesus. You are who you are through this gift and call of Jesus Christ!* (Romans 1:5-6)

In other words, you are who you are by the life of Jesus *and* the call of Jesus. You cannot have the abundant life of Christ without living the call of Christ to impact the lives of others. Your authentic life is forever bound together with other people.

The prophet Jeremiah told the exiled Israelites that they were to seek the peace and prosperity of the city of their captors *"because if it prospers, you too will prosper"* (Jer. 29:7 NIV). Isaiah wrote about this connection in chapter 58, saying that if you set the captive free, feed the hungry, and clothe the naked then *your* light will break forth. God knows you need other people. He even built your body to positively respond to the emotional experiences of appreciation, love, and caring—whether you are on the giving or receiving end of it, your heart, brain, hormones, and nervous system all respond with clear changes.

Finding the highest expression of authenticity begins with enjoying the loving relationship God is offering you, progresses into you loving yourself for who God made you to be, and then finally, through your connecting with others—a potpourri of people, all different from yourself—you are able to experience transformation.

People become the mirror that God uses so that you can see both your strengths and your weaknesses. When you are able to trust yourself, you will be able to trust others. It takes courage to keep showing up and putting your true self out there. It takes courage not to undermine or betray who you really are in search of approval. It might seem counterintuitive, but people need you just as you are, not as an imitation of someone else.

Many people are afraid to show their true self because of shame—they feel rejected simply because they reject themselves. When you are able to love yourself, you will draw to yourself others who love you. You must first, however, go to the Source of love. You must continue to tap into that love by opening your heart to other people drinking from the Source—a community of other believers. Begin to "graft yourself in"—get connected. There truly is power in numbers—supernatural power.

Margaret Wheatley, author of *Leadership and the New Science,* says that the quantum world has demolished the concept that people are unconnected individuals. She sees great benefit in our uniqueness to who we are together:

> With relationships we give up predictability and open up to potentials. We are as undefinable, unanalyzable, and bundled with potential as anything in the universe.... I have learned that great things are possible when we increase participation. I always want more people, from more diverse functions and places, to be there. I am always surprised by what people can create as they explore the webs of relation and caring that connect them.[2]

It's risky to expose yourself to the inevitability of pain inflicted by others in order to gain authenticity. Parker Palmer shares this secret: "No punishment anyone might inflict on them could possibly be worse than the punishment they inflict on themselves by conspiring in their own diminishment."[3] Greatness is risky. Take a chance!

> Integrity simply means not violating one's own identity. —Erich Fromm

As you journey toward authenticity, you must have a strong sense of identity—you must know who you are! Being confident in who God has called you to be is vital to the health of your soul and essential to your empowerment. Peter wrote, *"Once you had no identity as a people; now you are God's people"* (1 Pet. 2:10 NLT).

CHARACTERISTIC 24: IDENTITY

If I asked you the question, "Who are you?" would you answer with the role you play or the title you wear? So many people don't know who they are. People are always saying, "I'm trying to find myself; I don't know who I am; I don't know what I want; I don't know where I'm going." Perhaps you married hoping to find yourself. You went to college, identified a career, and had a family, but did you really find yourself? If you're like most people, other people have been telling you who you are all your life. But who does God say you are? Who did *He* create you to be? Pray about who God has called you to be—ask Him to show you your identity *in Him*, because when you have a sense of that, you will find the courage to dare to live authentically.

The challenge to live authentically is a call to everyone. Stop defining yourself by your past mistakes. Stop defining yourself by your roles and titles. Stop defining yourself by your feelings. Get to know who God created you to be so you can live life out loud. Jesus gave us some insight into this when He taught:

> *It's who you are and the way you live that count before God. Your worship must engage your spirit in the pursuit of truth. That's the kind of people the Father is out looking for: those who are simply and honestly themselves before Him…. Those who worship Him must do it out of their very being, their spirits, their true selves* (John 4:23-24).

Your authentic, divine self is the seed of greatness God put on the inside of you—the deposit God made when He formed *"Christ in you, the hope of glory"* (Col. 1:27 NKJV). Embrace the glory within you. Engage it and cultivate it by mindfully doing whatever you do to the glory of God. It is how you present your life as a living sacrifice—*"your reasonable service"*—that is the truest form of worship (see Rom. 12:1 NKJV).

Instead of viewing yourself from someone else's estimation of who you are, view yourself as God sees you. Don't strive to live up to anyone's expectations other than God's—this will empower you to indentify yourself based on your potential rather your past experiences. Too many people have become victims of identity theft. You must take your personal power back. You must take ownership for answering the question concerning who you are. Don't allow yourself to walk around with an inferiority complex as a result of comparing yourself with other people. This line from an old science fiction show is anything but fictional: "You are a true warrior, and as such, never allow the indulgence of self-doubt to cloud your vision." Eleanor Roosevelt said, "No one can make you feel inferior without your consent."

When Boaz asked Ruth who she was, she quickly responded, *"Sir, I am Ruth…and you are the relative who is supposed to take care of me. So spread the edge of your cover over me"* (Ruth 3:9 CEV). Her answer is pregnant with revelation. She communicated confidence in who she was and who she understood herself to be. When she identified herself by name, she was saying, "I know who I am." Her name represented everything she was—her image, character, reputation, habits, beliefs, customs, traditions, values, expectations, purpose, potential, temperament, personality, brand, leadership style, communication strategies, life skills, memories, experience, education, dreams, goals, and vision. These things combined created her character, attitude, perception, reputation, responses, social persona, and image. They drove her communication style and determined how she responded to crisis and how she thought every day. They colored her perception of her world and affected how people perceived her. This had a bearing on how far she progressed within her field, what opportunities presented themselves, and finally how she capitalized upon them.

In Ephesians you are told:

> *Throw off your old sinful nature and your former way of life, which is corrupted by lust and deception. Instead, let the Spirit renew your thoughts and attitudes. Put on your new nature, created to be like God—truly righteous and holy* (Ephesians 4:22-24 NLT).

In Christ you have been given a new nature—an entirely new genetic code. According to Second Corinthians, *"Anyone who belongs to Christ has become a new person. The old life is gone; a new life has begun!"* (2 Cor. 5:17 NLT). Galatians 6:15 states that *"what counts is whether we have been transformed into a new creation"* (NLT).

What counts is whether or not your identity—your perception of yourself—is defined by God. Allow yourself to be defined by your Creator, to live into that image—to be informed and transformed by the knowledge of all God has created you to become. At the very end of the New Testament, we read that God has *"made us kings and priests...and we shall reign on the earth"* (Rev. 5:10 NKJV).

If you are to fulfill your destiny of reigning on this earth as a king and priest, you must be *"constantly renewed in the spirit of your mind"* (Eph. 4:23 AMP). Only by constant and continual renewal of your spirit, soul, and mind will you be able to change your beliefs about the capacity you carry for greatness.

- What does "greatness" look like to you?

- If you were truly living as a king and priest, or even simply as a "new creation in Christ," how would that look? How would it feel? How would you be different?

I like how Jesus summed it up:

In a word, what I'm saying is, Grow up. You're kingdom subjects. Now live like it. Live out your God-created identity. Live generously and graciously toward others, the way God lives toward you (Matthew 5:48).

"Live out your God-created identity!" Get a vision for your God-created identity and write down everything that you see. *"You have begun to live the new life, in which you are being made new and are becoming like the One who made you"* (Col. 3:10 NCV).

Your identity and your success go hand in hand. Many people sacrifice their identities by not doing what they really want to do. And that's why they're not successful. —Lila Swell

Day Twenty-five

Becoming

I am happy in my own skin. Jesus loves me, and I
have a future with Him. I want to be totally me, so
that when I'm with the Lord face to face, it is my
own life that I lay down and not the prefabrication
of one who always tried to be somebody else.
—Luci Swindoll

It is said that if you catch a small shark and confine it,
it will stay a size proportionate to the aquarium where
it lives; but if you turn it loose in the vastness of the
ocean, the same shark will grow to eight feet long. Jump
out of the aquarium of limited beliefs and start swimming
in the ocean of unlimited possibilities. God has a much
larger dream for you than you can even imagine; your purpose has been woven into the very fabric of your being.
You were never intended to live small, but to grow into the
vastness of potential the entire universe offers. But to be
seen by the world can be frightening. So you build walls
of protection and hunker down under the radar screen of
God's eye. At least that's what you think. It didn't work for
Adam and Eve, and it won't work for you either. The walls
you build to keep others out also keep you boxed in. The
apostle Paul described God's plan this way:

*I can't tell you how much I long for you to enter this wide-
open, spacious life. We didn't fence you in. The smallness*

you feel comes from within you. Your lives aren't small, but
you're living them in a small way.... Open up your lives.
Live openly and expansively! (2 Corinthians 6:11-13)

Staying where you are is neither possible nor normal.
Those in search of purpose and authenticity have a drive
to grow continually beyond where they currently are. Dr.
Henry Cloud says that people with this "characteristic
trait leave a wake of making things bigger and better over
time."[1] He goes on to provide from the laws of physics the
necessary ingredients for growth of anything in the created world: 1) connection to energy sources outside itself;
and 2) "templates of information and structure that mold
the direction of their growth."[2]

God is an endless source of power for becoming your
true self, the authentic you God is waiting to reveal. Fasting
positions your heart and mind to be expanded as you throw
off those things that are clogging up your soul—then you
will have room to receive the power the Holy Spirit makes
available to you. Energy also comes from enlisting the
help of others like coaches, counselors, spiritual directors,
and empowerment groups. It's when you open yourself up
to people who will push you to greater heights that real
change happens.

The template of growth is first of all Jesus Christ. You
are being conformed into Christ's likeness, which is the
very image of God the Father. Secondly, you are becoming
the true person God had in mind before the beginning
of time, as described in Psalm 139. But, you are not yet
there. God always creates capacity and then invites you to
live into it. He understands that you will never grow unless
you attempt things that you cannot do, take on challenges

that seem impossible, and stretch your faith to accommodate your desire.

That's the picture of God's pulling Abraham to become his true self. He appeared to Abraham and spoke capacity by blessing him. He called him to leave his past, creating a space for new knowledge of God. He gave him a new name, changing it from Abram to Abraham, which reflected his future as the father of many nations. Then He gave Abraham the opportunity to fill that capacity to the full and live into that challenge by letting go of his only connection to that future when He asked him to sacrifice Isaac. God provided at every step for Abraham's future identity and He will do it for you, too!

> Find a purpose in life so big it will challenge every capacity to be at your best. —David O. McKay

An understanding of purpose is essential for authentic living, not only understanding your divine purpose overall, but also living purposefully—or being purpose-minded. In other words, there is living true to your calling and assignment in a general sense, but there is also being purposeful in regards to everything you do. It is a mindset as much as it is a discipline.

CHARACTERISTIC 25: PURPOSE

Living purposefully is a lifestyle. Paul said it this way:

Look carefully then how you walk! Live purposefully and worthily and accurately, not as the unwise and witless, but as wise (sensible, intelligent people)...do not be vague and thoughtless and foolish, but understanding and firmly grasping what the will of the Lord is (Ephesians 5:15,17 AMP).

God created you on purpose for a purpose. Purpose is the reason for you being on this earth. Barry Munro said, "You are only as strong as your purpose, therefore let us choose reasons to act that are big, bold, righteous and eternal." It is up to you to be purposeful in understanding and firmly grasping what that purpose is. You must be intentional, deliberate, circumspect, and mindful. People look far and wide to discover purpose, but the answers are right in your back yard.

I recently read a story about discovering purpose. It went something like this:

One day a woodcutter took his grandson into the forest for his first experience in selecting and cutting an oak tree. These they would later sell to the boat builders. As they walked along, the woodcutter explained that the purpose of each tree is contained in its natural shape: some are straight for planks, some have the proper curves for the ribs of a boat, and some are tall for masts. The woodcutter told his grandson that by paying attention to the details of each tree, and with experience in recognizing these characteristics, someday he too might become the woodcutter of the forest.

A little way into the forest, the grandson saw an old oak tree that had never been cut. The boy asked his grandfather if he could cut it down because it was useless for boat building—there were no straight limbs, the trunk was short and gnarled, and the curves were going the wrong way. "We could cut it down for firewood," the grandson said. "At least then it will be of some use to us." The woodcutter replied that for now they should be about their work cutting the proper trees for the boat builders; maybe later they could return to the old oak.

After a few hours of cutting the huge trees, the grandson grew tired and asked if they could stop for a rest in some cool shade. The woodcutter took his grandson over to the old oak tree where they rested against its trunk in the cool shade beneath its twisted limbs. After they had rested a while, the woodcutter explained to his grandson the necessity of attentive awareness and recognition of everything in the forest and in the world. Some things are readily apparent, like the tall, straight trees; other things are less apparent, requiring closer attention, like recognition of the proper curves in the limbs. And some things might initially appear to have no purpose at all, like the gnarled old oak tree. The woodcutter stated, "You must learn to pay careful attention every day so you can recognize and discover the purpose God has for everything in creation. For it is this old oak tree, which you so quickly deemed useless except for firewood, that now allows us to rest in the cool of the shade. Remember, grandson, not everything is as it first appears. Be patient, pay attention, recognize, and discover."

Don't let people cut you down or belittle you. Don't allow anyone to determine your purpose—they might mistake you for firewood instead of a shelter, or make you into a doormat or a punching bag. Dr. Myles Munro said, "Where purpose is not known, abuse is inevitable."

Everything and everyone in life has purpose. Jesus said, *"Pay close attention to what you hear. The closer you listen, the more understanding you will be given"* (Mark 4:24 NLT). It is up to you to press in to hear what God has purposed for you—and then to obey what you hear. Jesus went on to say, *"If you refuse to do your part, you cut yourself off from God's part"* (Matt. 6:15).

- Take time today to reflect on God's purposes and how those are reflected in your own. How intentionally are you pursuing this on a daily basis?

- Write down what you hear God saying about His purpose for you in the season you're in now. Pay close attention to what God's Spirit is speaking to yours. Remember, the closer you listen, the more understanding you will be given.

- What can you be doing more of to "do your part" in bringing God's purpose for your life to pass? What should you be doing less of? Heed this advice from Proverbs: *"Form your purpose by asking for counsel, then carry it out using all the help you can get"* (Prov. 20:18).

Be intentional. Be purpose-minded.

I pray that as a result of this *40 Day Soul Fast* God gives you a clearer understanding of what He has called you to do, as well as a greater capacity to do it. *"May He grant you according to your heart's desire, and fulfill all your purpose"* (Ps. 20:4 NKJV).

The soul which has no fixed purpose in life is lost; to be everywhere, is to be nowhere. —Michel Eyquem De Montaigne

Becoming

Before I formed you in the womb I knew [and] approved of you [as My chosen instrument], and before you were born I separated and set you apart, consecrating you (Jeremiah 1:5 AMP).

Week Six

The Power of Words: Healing the Hole in Your Soul

Day Twenty-six

Eating

Not that Christians don't own and read their Bibles. And not that Christians don't believe that their Bibles are the Word of God. What is neglected is reading the Scriptures formatively, reading in order to live. —Eugene Peterson[1]

"Eating your words" is a familiar euphemism and may seem a strange topic when speaking of fasting. Eugene Peterson brilliantly likens the Hebrew word for *meditating* to a dog gnawing on a bone, savoring it as he works it over and over. Scripture records several events where great men like Ezekiel, Jeremiah, and John are described as eating a book or a scroll, representing taking the very words of God into the body, mind, and spirit.

Your life is also a book, one written by God. Eating and meditating on God's Word, letting it form in you and shape you into a conduit for His purposes in the world, demands focused attention on the diet of your mind—not a simple task in a world full of words.

Words, words, words. Advertising on the side of a bus, a banner behind an airplane or affixed to a cart in the grocery store. Your ears are bombarded all day long with words—meetings, children, radio, television, telephones, or iPods. Conversation flies at speeds that could break the sound barrier—no time to think before you say the next thing and little time to process the implications and meaning of the words that get deposited in your mind without your permission.

The proliferation of words makes it easy to stop noticing them. However, words you take in subconsciously are no less dangerous in their spiritual power than the ones you *choose* to take in.

God created words—in the form of language, unspoken thoughts, internal images, and "pictures worth a thousand words"—as containers to fill with our faith. The whole universe and every living creature in it were brought into being by words. God thought it and spoke it and it was so. That's essentially what God is making reference to in Isaiah 55:

> *"For My thoughts are not your thoughts, nor are your ways My ways," declares the Lord. "For as the heavens are higher than the earth, so are My ways higher than your ways, and My thoughts than your thoughts"* (Isaiah 55:8-9 NKJV).

The word "higher" doesn't refer to a physical location but a way of operating. It means to imagine, plan, and invent—and then bring forth an intended conclusion. This passage of Scripture goes on to say that when God sends His word to Earth it will accomplish what He sends it to do. God's thoughts cannot be separated from His schematics, plans, inventions, designs, and actions to make it so.

You are created in His image, and part of that likeness is the power your words wield. Hebrews 11:3 states, *"The worlds were framed by the word of God, so that the things which are seen were not made of things which are visible"* (NKJV). Possibility, capacity, and systems are ingrained in God's speaking. Your words frame your world as well—although admittedly not in the same measure—still with great power and authority for those who work in union with Him. God has fixed the boundaries, and you operate within those borders with the faith you express with your words.

Proverbs 18:21 tells us that life and death are in the power of the tongue. James concurs, calling the tongue a fire and saying that it contaminates the whole body and sets *"the wheel of life on fire"* (James 3:6 BBE). He illustrated his point by relating the tongue to a bit in a horse's mouth or a rudder on a ship. Both determine the direction of the vessel. Your words establish the direction of your life as well, taking you down the road to authenticity or detouring you to mediocrity, or even immobilizing you altogether into a life of fear. Operate in the power of words by legislating, asking, sowing, and blessing.

> Without knowing the force of words, it is impossible to know men. —Confucius

Learning to live authentically is all about learning to be true to who you really are—it's about living congruently so that what you say and do align with your core values and divine nature. It's about being formed and molded into the divine blessing God created to be.

CHARACTERISTIC 26: INTEGRITY

Living with integrity is more than "moral rectitude"—it is also being true to your genuine essence as a unique reflection of God's glory.

What is in the book that God wrote about you—*"written not with ink but by the Spirit of the living God"* (2 Cor. 3:3)? In the Old Testament, David declared, *"God rewrote the text of my life when I opened the book of my heart to his eyes"* (Ps. 18:20 MSG).

Are you living according to the script God created for your life? You are a letter written by Christ (see 2 Cor. 3:3

CEV). Your life is a "wide open book" (Ps. 69:5)—so make sure you pay attention to what it is saying.

Paul told Timothy, *"Teach believers with your life: by word, by demeanor, by love, by faith, by integrity"* (1 Tim. 4:11 MSG).

What is your life saying about you?

The integrity of steel is determined by the stress and weight it is able to bear. When you are under pressure, what is revealed? Do you remain strong and immoveable when it comes to who God has called you to be?

Have you remained true to your purpose—to your passions? Have you been distracted or derailed by circumstances—or have you continued to actively pursue those things that make you feel most alive?

There is something God has hidden within you that may only be revealed through crisis or difficulty. Like a diamond that is formed under great pressure—or a stone made smooth by friction—or gold that is refined by fire. Whatever it is, it will be used to bless others.

- What are the circumstances in your life that are making you stronger? What is tempering you and testing your integrity?

- As a result of this refining process, write down what you know in your heart will be revealed. What treasure are you carrying on the inside of you that needs to find expression in the world around you?

He trained us first, passed us like silver through refining fires, brought us into hardscrabble country, pushed us to our very limit, road-tested us inside and out . . . finally he brought us to this well-watered place (Psalm 66:8 MSG).

Try not to become a man of success but rather try to become a man of value. —Albert Einstein

What you get in your life is not a result of what you want, it is a result of Who You Are. —Marlon Smith

Day Twenty-seven

Legislating

Prayer is the conduit through which power from
Heaven is brought to earth. —Ole Hallesby

Jesus said that the greatest faith He had ever seen on
Earth was that of a Gentile centurion—a soldier in the
service of his king. The story found in Matthew 8 says
that the centurion understood the power of words in legislating. Rather than have Jesus come and lay hands on his
sick servant, the soldier believed that Jesus, as a representative of His King, had the authority and power to speak
a word and the ordering of events and actions would take
place. Who wouldn't want that kind of power?

Moses spoke and ten plagues fell on the Egyptians.
Another time he spoke to a rock and water poured out to
quench the thirst of hundreds of thousands of people. Ezekiel spoke to a field of dry bones and they rose up and became
a mighty army. Elijah spoke and it didn't rain for three years
and then he spoke again and it did. After Peter and John
spoke, a man was healed. Proverbs 10:20 declares that the
"tongue of the righteous is as choice silver" (NASB). Silver is an
amazingly potent conductor of power. Each of the mere mortals mentioned above were used as potent conduits of Gods
power—conducting God's will *with words.*

You, like Adam and Eve, were created as a speaking
being, to rule and have governing power as a representative
of your King. That's what Peter wrote in his first letter:

You are the ones chosen by God, chosen for the high calling of priestly work, chosen to be a holy people, God's instruments to do His work and speak out for Him (1 Peter 2:9)

We are to *"display the virtues and perfections of Him Who called you"* (AMP). The King James Version of the same text calls you *"royal,"* and as such you have the right to legislate just like a king. You are an element in God's plan to reconcile the world back to Him. You do that by presenting your body parts as weapons of righteousness—including your mouth—so that as you speak you bring the will of God to Earth. Jesus taught the disciples to *declare* God's will be done on Earth—that the spiritual realm would manifest itself in the material realm.

Jesus demonstrated this power—but not before satan tried to use that power against Him during His 40 days in the desert by suggesting He speak to the stones to turn them into bread to satisfy His hunger. The use of His power was not the reason for Jesus' refusal, since not long after that He turned the water into wine by speaking. It wasn't even the fact that it would meet His own need, since He undoubtedly drank the wine He later produced, ate the bread He multiplied to feed the five thousand, and miraculously produced a coin in the mouth of a fish to pay His taxes. Jesus refused to do what satan suggested because His Father would not be worshiped and praised, or as Peter put it, His virtues would not be made clear.

You will never live up to your potential without the ability to legislate with your words in the spiritual realm, bringing God's will for you to Earth and warring against the forces of evil that would hinder it. But God isn't going to entrust such power to anyone unwilling to take responsibility for a heart free of wrong motivations, for out of the heart the mouth speaks.

Dr. Caroline Leaf's brain research shows that power for living comes from congruence. She states:

> Your words have to be backed up with honesty and integrity—*what in psychological terms is called congruence. What you do and say on the outside must reflect what you think on the inside. A lack of congruence causes stress and affects the way information is processed and memory is built.*[1]

A heart aligned with God leads to right thoughts and words, which open the door to power that can bring water from a rock. You have the authority and power to legislate on behalf of the King of kings! Getting a hold of that one truth will change your life forever.

When I ask my audiences, "What one thing can you change that will change everything?"—*this* is the one thing. Grab hold of your God-given ability to legislate through what you speak. I promise it will change your future.

> Handle them carefully, for words have more power than atom bombs. —Pearl Strachan

Over the course of the past five weeks, we have talked a great deal about your power—and essentially your obligation—to choose and decide for yourself whether or not you will live authentically and true to your divine nature. Do you realize the responsibility you have to the world to become who God is calling you to be?

CHARACTERISTIC 27: RESPONSIBILITY

It is up to you to guard your heart, govern your mindset, harness your thoughts, discipline your behavior, and direct your words. *You* must take responsibility. No one else can take responsibility for your life, your purpose, or your destiny other than you.

Take ownership of your potential—of your strengths, gifts, and calling—and take ownership of your weaknesses, mistakes, and even failures. In whatever area you have failed, own it, address it, embrace it as a priceless lesson, and move on.

Responsibility is simply your ability to respond. God has given you the ability to respond to not only your own personal experiences, but also to the circumstances around you. In addition to that, He has given you the capacity to respond to Him and to His Holy Spirit.

The degree to which you respond to God and to His call on your life will determine the degree to which you live authentically. Likewise, the degree to which you take responsibility for your own destiny will determine the degree to which you fulfill your purpose and maximize your potential.

Are you called to make a difference in this world? Are you called to make a lasting impact? Become someone God can rely on to be responsive and then take that responsibility seriously. Embrace *"the special responsibility of extending His grace"* (Eph. 3:2 NLT). *"If God has given you leadership ability, take the responsibility seriously"* (Rom. 12:8 NLT). Jesus said, *"A faithful, sensible servant is one to whom the master can give the responsibility of managing"* (Luke 12:42 NLT). Are you a faithful, sensible servant of God?

- What are the abilities God has given you? How well are you stewarding them?

246

- Has God called you to be a leader? Of course
  He has! The question is: How are you taking
  responsibility for fulfilling that call?

When you appear before the Lord, which all of us will, this is what He will ask you. I pray you will be among those who hear, *"Well done good and faithful servant!"* (Matt. 25:21 NKJV). Remember, you alone are responsible for not doing what you know you should.

Accept responsibility for your life. Know that it is you who will get you where you want to go, no one else.
—Les Brown

They heard the alarm but ignored it, so the responsibility is theirs. If they had listened...they could have saved lives (Ezekiel 33:5).

Day Twenty-eight

Asking

*We unlock change in our lives and in our world
when we choose to do God's will in God's way...
and it all begins with asking.* —Bruce Wilkerson

I once dated someone who had a problem with asking for directions. And you guessed it—we were always lost. We all have our stories of individuals too proud to ask. The Bible says, *"ask, and it will be given"* (Matt. 7:7; Luke 11:9 NASB). That is both a promise and a spiritual law. Sometimes we curse the answers we receive in life, not knowing that it is not the answer that is at fault, but the question. I call this, "The power of the question." Learn how to use this law to your advantage. It has been stated that the best time to ask questions, especially if you are trying to solve a problem, is to ask when you're open to receive answers. Asking questions is a form of active inquiry, whereby you create a relational culture of dynamic dialogues, discovery, learning, growth, exchange, and mindshare.

Asking is probably the most frequent form your words take in your relationship with God. You undoubtedly have asked for protection, blessing, counsel, and a host of other things for your life and the lives of those you care about. God does not begrudge your asking; He invites it. As a matter of fact, Scripture says that you have not because you ask not, and that you should, with prayer and supplication, make your requests known to God (see James 4:2; Phil. 4:6). In First Chronicles 4:9-10, a man by the name of Jabez boldly asked God to increase his territory and to bless him—and God did.

Even Jesus is seen asking throughout the Gospels. In Luke 2, Jesus is found in the Temple at the age of 12, asking the teachers to tell Him what they know about the Scriptures. He asked the blind man what he wanted Him to do for him, and when the woman with the issue of blood touched Him in the midst of a huge crowd, Jesus asked, "Who touched Me?" He spent His last few hours on Earth asking the Father for love, peace, joy, and unity among His disciples, for the cup of suffering to pass if possible, and for forgiveness for those who crucified Him. So Jesus obviously believed there was a purpose to asking of the Father. He didn't have a "what will be, will be" attitude like many today.

God has given you the right to approach Him with bold confidence and persistence, believing that He is good and knows how to give good gifts. That's the purpose of the parable told in Luke 11, where Jesus is teaching the disciples about asking. He tells them:

> *Ask, and it will be given to you; seek, and you will find; knock, and it will be opened to you. For everyone who asks, receives; and he who seeks, finds; and to him who knocks, it will be opened* (Luke 11:9-10 NASB).

Sink that deep into your mind!

Jesus illustrated the point by telling of a man who persistently asked his neighbor late at night for a loaf of bread, stating the man would surely get up and give him what the neighbor asked for if only he could sleep! He then said something that would be easy to miss and is critical to understanding the power of asking:

> *If you then, being evil, know how to give good gifts to your children, how much more will your Father who is in*

heaven give what is good [the Holy Spirit] *to those who ask Him!* (Matthew 7:11 NASB)

The Holy Spirit, often described as bread, is the fulfillment of everything you could ask for. He is the *"one thing"* David said in Psalm 27:4 that he desired and would seek. If that answer doesn't seem like it would meet your need then check out Revelation 5 where it describes the seven dimensions of the Spirit: *"power and riches and wisdom and might and honor and glory and blessing"* (Rev. 5:12 NASB). Would any of those make a difference in your situation? When you ask God for something in your life, it is His own Presence He sends—because there is absolutely nothing that is unavailable to you by His Spirit. In His Presence you find healing, wisdom, and *"fullness of joy"* (Ps. 16:11 NASB). God is more than ready to give beyond what you can ask or think, but you must first ask.

Henry Blackaby tells of his little church community in Canada who gathered to ask God to do bigger things than they could do alone. They took Daniel 3:17 to heart: *"Our God whom we serve is able...and He will"* (NASB). They wondered if they had the ability to do what God wanted to do through them. Blackaby said, "We sensed that this was the wrong question. The right question was this: Had God revealed His will for us? And if so, would we believe, obey, and trust Him?"[1]

Think big thoughts! Ask God, and He will!

God is willing to walk the earth again incarnate in us. —Eugenia Price

Sometimes the thing that keeps people from daring to live more authentically is their lack of vision—or their inability to see future possibilities for their lives. They get locked into a role or self-concept that is limiting—they become conditioned to portray a certain image or to stay within certain boundaries. These roles, self-concepts, or boundaries are often falsely imposed and can be deceiving.

As we journey toward authenticity, we are striving to peel away the falsehoods, façades, and other fetters that keep us from maximizing our true potential.

CHARACTERISTIC 28: POTENTIAL

Potential is unused and unrealized power to do and to become. And that's what this soul fast is all about—building your capacity for the great things God has in store for you. Satirist Philip Adams has been quoted as saying, "It seems to me that people have vast potential. Most people can do extraordinary things if they have the confidence or take the risks. Yet most people don't. They sit in front of the telly and treat life as if it goes on forever." Refuse to be among those who never explore the hidden potential that lies deep within—refuse to sit in front of the television being entertained by other people's success. When you muster up the courage to leave the shoreline of comfort and familiarity, you can become all that you are destined to be. Motivational speaker and author Rex Crain has said, "You can never become who you've been destined to become until you lose who you used to be."

What is keeping you from total expression of all that you were meant to be, to do, and to accomplish? What are the weights, doubts, fears, and other encumbrances keeping you from fully expressing your divine self?

Take a lesson from Paul, who said:

> *None of these things move me, neither count I my life dear*
> *unto myself, so that I might finish my course with joy, and*

the ministry, which I have received of the Lord Jesus (Act 20:24 KJV).

Another translation says, *"the work assigned me by the Lord"* (NLT), and another says, *"the work that the Lord Jesus gave me"* (NCV).

What is the work the Lord has given you? What has He assigned you to do? You will have to answer these questions if you are to maximize your potential in that area. Yes, you have the potential to do all sorts of things, but you need to focus on the thing God has assigned you alone to do. Understand what your assigned "craft" is—and then master it!

Identify the gifts God has placed within you and invest in developing them. This should be a priority. In fact, I would call it "mission critical"—as Paul said, *"The most important thing is that I complete my mission"* (Acts: 20:24 NCV). This, after all, is the work assigned you!

- Ask God, "What is my assignment?"

- Ask yourself, "What have I invested in maximizing my potential in that area?"

- Envision what your potential maximized would look like. Now, imagine how it might look with God working in and through you! Ask God to show you, and then ask Him to do it!

No eye has seen, no ear has heard, and no mind has imagined what God has prepared for those who love Him (1 Corinthians 2:9 NLT).

Man's main task in life is to give birth to himself, to become what he potentially is. The most important product of his effort is his own personality. —Erich Fromm

Look well to yourself [to your own personality]…persevere in these things [hold to them], for by so doing you will save both yourself and those who hear you (1 Timothy 4:16 AMP).

Day Twenty-nine

Sowing

Anyone can count the seeds in an apple, but only God can count the number of apples in a seed.
—Robert Schuller

There is an abundance of wisdom in God's Word about the laws of sowing and reaping. One of the most quoted is Galatians 6:7: *"Whatsoever a man sows, that he will also reap"* (NKJV). Laws are true in the natural world no matter who applies them. They are active in both the seen and unseen worlds. The law of gravity, for example, is not seen, but the results certainly are. Charles Reade described another unseen law: "Sow a thought, and you reap an act; sow an act, and you reap a habit; sow a habit, and you reap a character; sow a character, and you reap a destiny."

If you are to fulfill your destiny and become your authentic self, the law of sowing and reaping must be mastered, beginning with your thoughts and your words. You'll hear tomorrow about words that you speak to others, but today focus on words you say to yourself, even if only in your mind.

Paul wrote to the Corinthians that God gives seed to the sower and bread to the eater. A sower understands that what is sown, the seed, determines what will be harvested. If you have ever planted a seed in your garden that eventually overgrew and took over the entire plot, you have a picture of what negative thoughts, words, and emotions do to your brain.

In her book, *Who Switched Off My Brain?*, Dr. Leaf states that those negative thoughts grow like trees, branching out into greater expanses. Hate, she discovered, takes over the mind, physically taking up space in your brain until it crowds out everything else. Her encouraging research also revealed that when you begin to sow good thoughts and speak positive words to yourself in your mind, the new pathways actually overlay the old ones, until finally the positive attitudes dominate.[1]

A sower knows that the soil makes all the difference. Your character is like soil for seed. Dallas Willard describes character as a readiness to act. In other words, you will respond in situations according to your character, and your mind is part of that readiness. God is going to give you new ideas and new visions when the soil of your mind is ready and prepared. The parable of the sower illustrated in Matthew 13 describes ground that wasn't ready for the seed. Your mind must be prepared and in agreement with who God says you are so that you can take the land of your destiny.

The story of the 12 spies Moses sent into the Promised Land in Numbers 13 is an example of what happens when God is ready to give His people what He has promised and their character opens or shuts that door. Ten of the spies had unprepared minds and two were fully ready to receive what God wanted to give them. The ten saw themselves as grasshoppers, totally disconnected from the truth of who God had already said they were. They died in the desert, placeless and devoid of purpose. The other two, Joshua and Caleb, had received the same truth, but planted it firm in their thinking and were ready to act, to take the land of promise. They had a full life of leadership, prosperity, and legacy.

Sow truth in your mind and prepare the soil. God's Word is truth. Don't just put a little in your mind, but sow bountifully. That's what Second Corinthians reminds you to do: "A *stingy planter gets a stingy crop; a lavish planter gets a lavish crop"* (2 Cor. 9:6). Sow your thoughts lavishly, then reap your destiny lavishly!

> He who would be useful, strong, and happy must cease to be a passive receptacle for the negative, beggarly, and impure streams of thought; and as a wise householder commands his servants and invites his guests, so must he learn to command his desires and to say, with authority, what thoughts he shall admit into the mansion of his soul. —James Allen

CHARACTERISTIC 29: IMPECCABILITY

Impeccability. I love this word. I love this characteristic. Impeccability is what kept satan from having any power over Jesus (see John 14:30 NLT). Where sin leads to defeat and death, impeccability leads to victory and increasingly abundant life.

Impeccability has traditionally been defined as "free from sin." That hardly seems achievable for us mere mortals. Not to mention the Bible tells us *"all have sinned and fall short of the glory of God"* (Rom. 3:23 NIV). No one is perfect in that regard except for Christ.

So how do we adopt this characteristic into our everyday lives? I think of John 1:47 where Jesus said of Nathanael, *"Here is an Israelite indeed…in whom there is no guile"* (John 1:47 AMP). Or, as other translations say, *"no deceit"* (NKJV), *"nothing false"* (NCV), and *"a man of complete integrity"* (NLT). In other words, a man who is honest, transparent, has nothing to hide, who is living life inside out, a man who is living authentically, *"free of error, mixed motives, or hidden agendas"* (1 Thess. 2:3).

Authenticity has to do with honesty—do you always speak the truth? Do you say one thing when you mean another or misrepresent what you are truly feeling or thinking? The Bible speaks of one thing alone that makes a person perfect, and that is perfectly true words. James wrote, *"If anyone does not stumble in word, he is a perfect man"* (James 3:2 NKJV). Or, as *The Message* translation puts it, *"If you could find someone whose speech was perfectly true, you'd have a perfect person, in perfect control of life."*

Interestingly, I discovered impeccability in regards to the use of words was a concept referenced in the ancient traditions of the Toltecs, a pre-Aztecan culture.

"The strongest intent of the Toltec warrior," writes Allan Hardman in *The Everything Toltec Wisdom Book*, "is to be impeccable with his word. For the Toltecs, to be impeccable with the word means to not use it against one's self. The warrior is always on guard against negative self-talk, self-judgment, worry, gossip, and other fear-based uses of words."[2] To be impeccable with your word, then, means to not use it in any way that would hurt you.

- How have you used words against yourself?

- How "free of error, mixed motives, or hidden agendas" are you living? How transparent is your life and speech?

Would Jesus say of you, "Look, there goes a person in whom there is no guile"?

Be impeccable with your word. Speak with integrity. Say only what you mean. Avoid using the word to speak against yourself or to gossip about others. Use the power of your word in the direction of truth and love. —Miguel Angel Ruiz

Dare to be true. Nothing can need a lie: a fault which needs it most, grows two thereby. —George Herbert

Don't say anything you don't mean. ...You only make things worse when you lay down a smoke screen of pious talk, saying, "I'll pray for you," and never doing it, or saying, "God be with you," and not meaning it. You don't make your words true by embellishing them with religious lace. In making your speech sound more religious, it becomes less true. Just say "yes" and "no." When you manipulate words to get your own way, you go wrong (Matthew 5:33).

Day Thirty

Blessing

Words of love and affirmation are like bread. We need them each day, over and over. They keep us alive inside. —Henri Nouwen

In earlier reflections we considered this verse:

But you are a special people, a holy nation, priests and kings, a people given up completely to God, so that you may make clear the virtues of Him who took you out of the dark into the light of heaven (1 Peter 2:9 BBE).

That day the focus was on your kingly legislating on God's behalf. But what about the idea of being a priest as Peter referred to in the same passage?

The priest in the Old Testament had the responsibility to first bless the Name of God and then to bear the needs of the people to Him, asking for blessing and provision. He combined his words with hope and expectation that God would, in response to those words of blessing and praise, act on their behalf—that He would bless them.

God said that when He speaks, His words do not return to Him without accomplishing what He sent them to do. In the beginning, He blessed Adam and Eve, instructing them to be fruitful and multiply, to subdue and rule the Earth. That wasn't just a command, however, but His blessing within which contained the capacity to accomplish His vision for their life.

Jesus released words of blessing just before He returned to Heaven. Luke 24:50-51 shows Him leading the disciples to Bethany and then lifting His hands as He spoke words of blessing on them and gave them the commission to go and make disciples. Those words were not simply benign puffs of air, but contained life-giving power to forward them toward their fulfillment and purpose.

You have the power to use your words to accomplish the same thing in the lives that God brings across your path—to speak life-giving words that forward yourself and others along. Words of encouragement, identity, vision, kindness, and purpose, showing compassion and gentleness even to your enemies or others who are undeserving or ungrateful will make a difference. It will expand your capacity for greatness when you make room for them at the table of life by inviting their uniqueness instead of trying to mold them into someone they are not. When you are able to do this, you too will be multiplied. Unlike the laws of sowing and reaping, blessing supersedes natural law and moves you into the realm of the miraculous, the unexpected.

It is written in Ecclesiastes 11:1 that if you *"cast your bread upon the waters...you will find it after many days"* (NKJV). What a strange thing to say. How could you possibly throw bread into water and ever expect to find it again, let alone receive a harvest of any value? Actually the word *bread* is better understood as what some call bread-corn, or seed, and implies that like bread, it is the necessity of life. The idea here is that there are no expectations when the sower sows the seed. Where the water will carry it is totally out of the hands of the one who released it.

That's the picture of your words set free on God's behalf. Your seed, or words, are the necessity of life to others—they are bread as Nouwen said. Don't withhold them. When God moves you by His Spirit to speak blessing, do it. You have no way of knowing what harvest God is going to bring from them. Proverbs 15:23 (WEB) says, *"Joy comes to a man with the reply of his mouth. How good is a word at the right time!"* Release your words of blessing in hope and faith that God will bring a harvest of joy for you and the love of God to the receiver. As is true with the law of sowing and reaping, you always reap more than you sow!

> If I choose to bless another person, I will always end up feeling more blessed. —Marianne Williamson

In the last few days, we've talked about *responsibility, potential,* and *impeccability.* Today, I want to talk to you about *compassion*—because without this characteristic, you will have a difficult time fully walking in any of the other characteristics of an authentic person.

CHARACTERISTIC 30: COMPASSION

Compassion is love in action. It comprises mercy, kindness, generosity, justice, and patience. It represents the nature of God—*"Your God, is above all a compassionate God"* (Deut. 4:29).

Throughout Scripture we are told, *"God is gracious and compassionate,"* *"a forgiving God, gracious and compassionate, incredibly patient, with tons of love"* (2 Chron. 30:9 NIV; Neh. 9:16). And then we are told to be just like Him: *"So be merciful (sympathetic, tender, responsive, and compassionate) even as your Father is"* (Luke 6:36 AMP).

Compassion can be defined as "deep awareness of the suffering of another coupled with the wish to relieve it—the humane quality of understanding the suffering of others and wanting to do something about it."[1] It is the quality that causes us to take on the cares and concerns of those around us. It's what binds us together as "one body"—to share one another's burdens and "weep with those who weep." It is what makes us humans *humane.*

Moreover, compassion represents God's heart for social justice. At the tail end of the Old Testament we read:

> *The message hasn't changed. God-of-the-Angel-Armies said then and says now: "Treat one another justly. Love your neighbors. Be compassionate with each other. Don't take advantage of widows, orphans, visitors, and the poor"* (Zechariah 7:7).

Paul wrote that being compassionate made us useful: *"Become useful and helpful and kind to one another…compassionate, understanding, loving-hearted"* (Eph. 4:32 AMP). Peter wrote, *"Finally, all of you, be like-minded, be sympathetic, love one another, be compassionate and humble"* (1 Pet. 3:8 NIV).

I encourage you today to check your compassion meter. Open your heart and mind to those in need around you and explore how you might respond to those needs. Speak a blessing into the lives of everyone you encounter.

- Think of someone you normally don't have patience for, and speak a blessing over him or her now.

- The next time you come across a person less fortunate, stop and bless them with your words. You might not have the money or time to invest, but you always have a kind word— and there is no better investment than that.

What better way is there to share the love of God than to bless others with your words? That is how you shine light into dark places! And how that light is reflected back to you: *"Light arises in the darkness for the...compassionate and righteous"* (Ps. 112:4 NKJV).

Too often we underestimate the power of a touch, a smile, a kind word, a listening ear, an honest accomplishment, or the smallest act of caring, all of which have the potential to turn a life around. —Leo Buscaglia

But He's already made it plain how to live, what to do, what God is looking for in men and women. It's quite simple...be compassionate and loyal in your love, and don't take yourself too seriously (Micah 6:8).

Week Seven

The Power of Doing: God's Chosen Fast

Day Thirty-one

Helping

The world needs dreamers and the world needs doers. But above all, the world needs dreamers who do. —Sarah Ban Breathnach

The balance of being and doing is as old as Adam and Eve in the Garden. The debate over whether one should focus on who they are or what they do is as ancient as the Torah itself. God created both, and they cannot be easily separated. In a previous week you looked at who you are regarding your identity apart from what you do—this week you will focus on the *do* part of you.

What you do affects the life of your soul as much as your thoughts or words. You were created and put on this earth *to do* something, just as were Adam and Eve. After God blessed Adam and Eve, He told them to get going—to be productive by managing all that He had created and increasing it. There should be little doubt that basking in a stream and eating grapes all day wasn't what God had in mind. The famous quote, "God is a verb" by Buckminster Fuller paints a picture of God Himself as always doing. Jesus said His Father was always at work.

Because you were made in His image, you might wonder if God expects more from you than going to church, studying the Bible, and praying. The answer is *yes!* Too often there is more talk than action. Paul warned Timothy why that is such a problem:

Concentrate on doing your best for God, work you won't be ashamed of.... Stay clear of pious talk that is only talk. Words are not mere words, you know. If they're not backed by a godly life, they accumulate as poison in the soul (2 Timothy 2:15-17).

Detoxing your soul must deal with the poison accumulated from words with no action to back them up. Living your authentic life is a journey of exploits, not a destination.

David Allen, author of the best-selling book *Getting It All Done*, says that just taking the next step of what you already know to do increases productivity and your ability to make things happen, impacting your thoughts with a rise in self-esteem and a constructive outlook on life. The Random Acts of Kindness Foundation has published numerous studies that show helping someone else actually changes your body chemistry.

For example, a 10-year study of 2,700 men found that those who did regular volunteer work had death rates two and one-half times lower than those who didn't. Could it be that research simply backs up what God has already invested into the way the universe operates? Hebrews promises blessings from God if you take the ideas, anointing, and visions that come down from Heaven and do something with them:

For the ground that drinks the rain which often falls upon it and brings forth vegetation useful to those for whose sake it is also tilled, receives a blessing from God (Hebrews 6:7 NASB).

Dallas Willard confirms that you can only know the regular and reliable presence of God's Kingdom in your life by taking action, now: "We make our moments divine by not postponing acting for Him, but by stepping in action now beyond what is regarded as safe and proper, into situations where only God can help us." Taking action doesn't imply forcing your way on others or seeing yourself as the person with all the answers. Helping will require you to believe the best of people. Be prepared to listen before acting. But do act. Do something. Donate food to a food bank; build a house with Habitat for Humanity; purchase fair trade products; or get involved with feeding the homeless. Start somewhere and see where God will take you. Act now on what you know by partnering, continuing, prioritizing, and willing.

> To believe in men is the first step toward helping them. —Walt Disney

Akin to showing compassion is showing respect. Without the ability to respect the rights, opinions, and differences of others, you won't be able to show compassion toward those who might not think or look or behave like you.

CHARACTERISTIC 31: RESPECT

The Bible tells us to *"show respect for all people"* (1 Pet. 2:17 NCV) and *"show respect and honor to them all"* (Rom. 13:7 NCV).

Respect can be defined as "to hold in esteem or honor." In many cases throughout the Bible, it is used interchangeably with the word *honor.* We are told to honor our parents, the elderly, and those in authority—as well as one another. It is part and parcel of walking in love: *"Be devoted to one another in love. Honor one another above yourselves"* (Rom. 12:10 NIV).

If you dare to live authentically, you will be required to demonstrate honor and humility. In fact, without developing this trait, you will never be able to show the Lord your God the honor and respect He seeks from those who love Him. The Bible says that to honor the poor and elderly and outcast is to honor Him.

God is a God of honor. He is honorable and worthy of honor. So, too, should you be in all you do. Be imitators of your Heavenly Father and show respect for not only those in authority, but for those who seem inferior or unworthy.

Imitate God who *"rekindles burned-out lives with fresh hope, restoring dignity and respect to their lives—a place in the sun!"* (1 Sam. 2:6). You may be instrumental in helping others embrace their own authenticity—and the more people dare to live authentically, the better the world will be!

If you want to be respected, you must show respect. This is why humility comes before honor. Those who are unable to honor and respect all people will themselves never become honorable. You cannot "demand" respect, but only "command" it by taking action on behalf of others.

- What one thing can you do today to honor someone?

- To what degree do you command respect? Are you a leader others look up to because you are respectful—as in "full of respect?"

Be reminded of the proverb which states, *"Leadership gains authority and respect when the voiceless poor are treated fairly"* (Prov. 29:14). In other words, be proactive in lending a helping hand.

There is no better way to thank God for your sight than by giving a *helping* hand to someone in the dark. —Helen Keller

Helping

Do what you can, with what you have, where you are.
—Theodore Roosevelt

Make the Master proud of you by being good citizens. Respect the authorities, whatever their level; they are God's emissaries for keeping order. It is God's will that by doing good, you might cure the ignorance of the fools who think you're a danger to society. Exercise your freedom by serving God, not by breaking the rules. Treat everyone you meet with dignity. Love your spiritual family. Revere God. Respect the government (1 Peter 2:13-17).

Day Thirty-two

Partnering

> Teamwork is the ability to work together toward a common vision; it is the fuel that allows common people to attain uncommon results. —Andrew Carnegie

With is a small but powerful concept. The whole Bible is made up of the story of God *with* humanity. God created Eve because He said that Adam should not be alone. He continued along that line of thinking until and beyond the birth of His own Son. When the angel appeared to Mary and told her she would have the long-awaited Messiah, he also declared that the Father had named Him *Emmanuel*, "God with us," continuing His promise to be with humanity. Jesus, *Emmanuel*, wisely chose not to be alone Himself, but partnered with 12 other men as He carried out His Father's will on Earth.

Synergy is a *with* concept. The power of synergy—a result of doing which is more than the sum of the parts—often accomplishes what dozens of individuals working alone cannot. A visible example of this is the Tower of Babel in Genesis 11. Even though it was clear that God wasn't pleased with the people, it still illustrates that people working together can do amazing things:

> *See, they are all one people and have all one language; and this is only the start of what they may do: and now it will not be possible to keep them from any purpose of theirs* (Genesis 11:6 BBE).

Your soul needs other people for many reasons. Wielding your shield of faith as you rush forward into your destiny may sound like something you can handle alone, but acts of faith often need companionship and even a whole social network. Chip Ingram describes the biblical idea of a shield of faith, saying that the shields of Roman soldiers were designed to be linked together so that a whole row of soldiers could move forward simultaneously. What a great picture of partnering with others to do life. Why would anyone want to make this journey alone?

Proverbs 20 explains another reason why it isn't a good idea to go it on your own: *"Though good advice lies deep within the heart, a person with understanding will draw it out"* (Prov. 20:5 NLT). You need to surround yourself with people of understanding to help draw out what God has planted deep within your soul to do, to see what you might miss, and to help you stay in touch with reality—not allowing yourself to be tricked into only seeing what you want to see. That type of relationship can only happen when there is great trust—when you know that people are loyal companions and have your back so you can relax.

David had such a friend and traveling companion in Jonathan. We read in First Samuel: *"The soul of Jonathan was joined with the soul of David, and David became as dear to him as his very life"* (1 Sam. 18:1 BBE). Choose wisely who you join yourself with, because research has proven that even people three degrees removed from you can have some influence on your happiness, health habits, and in other life-directing areas.

One survey looked at the factors that influence wellbeing, meaning your ability to feel safe and to be involved with a greater community. They found that your chances of sensing a thriving overall wellbeing are 63 percent higher if you live with someone who also does, and it goes down to only 20 percent if you don't. Similar findings showed up in other relationships they looked at, such as friendships and work associates. So consider carefully with whom you do life.

Finally, choose traveling companions with whom you can laugh. Laughter is the best medicine, washing your body and soul with feel-good chemicals—a true stress buster!

> We are all travelers in the desert of life and the best we can find in our journey is an honest friend.
> —Robert Louis Stevenson

Last week we focused on the power of our words, highlighting the authentic characteristics of impeccability, compassion, and respect—demonstrating that our words are simply a reflection of what is in our hearts. Beyond words is how we choose to behave—what we choose to do and the decisions we make every moment of every day.

CHARACTERISTIC 32: LOYALTY

Our choices and actions reflect a very important characteristic of living authentically—loyalty. How congruently are you living when it comes to what you do? I'm not referring to your profession, but your behavior. As you journey toward authenticity, you cannot separate the intents, motives, and desires residing within your heart from your behavior. Aligning your thoughts, words, and actions with your higher purpose—as well as the greater good—requires loyalty.

Loyalty is evidenced by singleness of heart. James talked about the *"double-minded man"* who should not expect to receive anything from God (James 1:8 NKJV). Instead, James wrote, *"when you ask him, be sure that your faith is in God alone"* (James 1:6 NLT). He went on to add:

> *Do not waver, for a person with divided loyalty is as unsettled as a wave of the sea that is blown and tossed by the wind…. Their loyalty is divided between God and the world, and they are unstable in everything they do* (James 1:6,8 NLT).

A person who is not loyal is unsettled and unstable. God cannot reward such a person. The prophet Samuel pointed out that, *"The Lord rewards us for the things we do right and for our loyalty"* (1 Sam. 26:23 NCV). The degree to which you show yourself loyal to God—faithful, obedient, and God-fearing—will determine to what extent you are able to live authentically.

Through the prophet Ezekiel, God said, *"I am the Lord [the Sovereign Ruler, Who calls forth loyalty and obedient service]"* (Ezek. 38:23 AMP). And in Psalms we read, *"My loyalty and love will be with him. Through Me he will be strong"* (Ps. 89:24 NCV).

In other words, the very nature of God's loyalty and love working in you will make you strong and position you for power. Proverbs states, *"Loyalty and truth keep a king in power; he continues to rule if he is loyal"* (Prov. 20:28 NCV). Proverbs also says that, *"Loyalty makes a person attractive"* (Prov. 19:22 NLT).

There is no going wrong for those who are loyal at heart.

- How is God's loyalty working in *and* through your life?

- In what areas might your loyalties be "divided"? What can you do to change that?

If you want to lock arms and do life with quality people of understanding who are trustworthy and loyal, you will have to prove yourself loyal.

> *Plant goodness, harvest the fruit of loyalty; plow the new ground of knowledge. Look for the Lord until He comes and pours goodness on you like water* (Hosea 10:12 NCV).

Loyalty is the pledge of truth to oneself and others.
—Ada Velez-Boardley

> *Don't lose your grip on Love and Loyalty. Tie them around your neck; carve their initials on your heart. Earn a reputation for living well in God's eyes and the eyes of the people* (Proverbs 3:3).

Day Thirty-three

Continuing

Miracles of grace must be the seals of our ministry; who can bestow them but the Spirit of God.
—C.H. Spurgeon

Stephen Covey is well known today for his phrase "to live, to love, to learn, to leave a legacy." It's true that God desires for the work of your hands to result in something that continues on after you are no longer on this Earth. What exactly lasts that long? Does that mean you are to build a structure for people to occupy, to create a foundation that funds good works, or, as most people think of it, to raise up many disciples for Christ? Only God knows the right answer for each individual, but one of the best criteria He gives you is that whatever you do in this life is to be done to His glory. That's what lasts!

Isaiah declared that he saw a vision of the whole Earth filled with God's glory. At least part of that is the work done by the hands of God's people on His behalf in a way that produces glory for God. Jesus said that what you do for the greatest and for "the least of these" counts—even a cup of cold water given to one who is thirsty is the same as giving Jesus Himself a drink.

You, like everyone else, have a longing for a sense of purpose and meaning—for having a hand in something that changes the world for good. No one wants to go to their grave without seeing God's miraculous power at work. Miracles come in all sizes. The time you spend to purify your soul and reconnect with the energizing power of God opens the door for you to act in such a way that others see God at work. That's a miracle.

Dr. Henry Cloud calls what you leave behind when you are with other people "your wake." It's the results of not just what you do, but how you do it. So ask yourself: Are people who interact with you more trusting, more hopeful, and more fulfilled for having been with you? Do you have credibility with others because they see you as sincerely caring about what's best for them? Do they become more like their true self or are they diminished and imprisoned? Do you produce fear or love in others?

Each person you touch will pass along the results of being with you to those they touch, so in essence, each action or word from you becomes part of your legacy, reaching beyond any present moment and continuing on when you are gone. Dr. Cloud proposes that the healing and wholeness of your own heart and soul brings the greatest "wake" for others and the greatest fulfillment for you. Otherwise you pass on your own dysfunction.

You may not yet be whom you long to become—your true self, complete and whole—but press on knowing that all of creation feels the same way—incomplete. And yet God is in the waiting:

> *Everything in creation is being more or less held back. God reins it in until both creation and all the creatures are ready and can be released at the same moment into the glorious times ahead. Meanwhile, the joyful anticipation deepens. All around us we observe a pregnant creation. The difficult times of pain throughout the world are simply birth pangs. But it's not only around us; it's within*

us. The Spirit of God is arousing us within. We're also feeling the birth pangs. These sterile and barren bodies of ours are yearning for full deliverance. That is why waiting does not diminish us, any more than waiting diminishes a pregnant mother. We are enlarged in the waiting. We, of course, don't see what is enlarging us. But the longer we wait, the larger we become, and the more joyful our expectancy (Romans 8:20-25).

Continue on! Things are happening in you that you can't see but are truer than true!

The whole point of being alive is to evolve into the complete person you were intended to be. —Oprah Winfrey

This week we are focusing on the power of doing. What we do is a result of the decisions we make and the actions we take as a result. You are always one decision away from changing the course of your life and from living the life of your dreams. Your choices and behaviors establish your credibility.

CHARACTERISTIC 33: CREDIBILITY

Credibility simply means "believability." Are you someone who says one thing and does another? Can people believe what you say? Without establishing your credibility—your believability—you will never be true to yourself. There's no deception worse than self-deception! You must hold yourself accountable for your own legitimacy, genuineness, and yes, authenticity. This is what lasting reputations are built upon.

You have heard it said that a person is only as good as his or her word. Make sure you don't "speak out of both sides of your mouth" or practice what some call "double speak"— this is the fruit of being double-minded, the detriments of which we spoke of yesterday. Psalm 15:4 talks about how those who honor God keep their promises even when it hurts them. That is how you establish credibility with yourself and with others—when you do what you say even if it hurts.

- *Consciously strive to create credibility.* Practice proven credibility boosters such as being honest, being on time, being a person of your word—being dependable.

- *What is your promise to the world?* Establishing credibility is only a means to an end, not the end itself. What can people count on you to do because you are here? What do you stand for? How will you leave your mark?

If you are to be successful in any arena or pursuit in life, you must be credible—or, as we said, believable—because ultimately *you* are the product. *You* are the dream, the service, the idea, the message, even the Gospel made flesh.

The father of modern advertising, Leo Burnett, who was named by *Time* magazine as one of the 100 most influential people of the twentieth century, once said, "The greatest thing to be achieved...in my opinion, is believability."

> The more you are willing to accept responsibility for your actions, the more credibility you will have.
> —Brian Koslow

Continuing

Remove impurities from the silver and the silversmith can craft a fine chalice; remove the wicked from leadership and authority will be credible and God-honoring (Proverbs 25:4-5).

Day Thirty-four

Prioritizing

> If then you are wise, you will show yourself rather as a reservoir than as a canal. A canal spreads abroad water as it receives it, but a reservoir waits until it is filled before overflowing, and thus without loss to itself it shares its superabundant water. —Bernard of Clairvaux[1]

Paul told Timothy that no soldier in active service should entangle himself in the affairs of everyday life. Makes you wonder if he had any idea of what today's world would look like. *Doing* is the normal mode of Western society. The culture is one of constant interaction—both at work and with friends and family. Information and new ideas flood in from all over the globe—which can be invigorating to your thought life, sparking dreams and plans for the future, but it can also mean taking on too much and ending up with mediocre results or being so overwhelmed you feel constantly defeated.

The discipline of choosing and prioritizing prevents the entanglement that Paul had in mind. It frees your mind and heart to focus on what God has put there. Productivity guru David Allen says that we are "allowing in huge amounts of information and communication from the outer world and generating an equally large volume of ideas and agreements with ourselves and others from our inner world. And we are not well equipped to deal with this huge number of internal and external commitments."[2] In other words, you need to learn to say "No!" even to some good things.

It takes disciplined thinking to make choices and create boundaries that leave space and time in your life for the truly important things. Temperance, moderation, and self-control will help free you from instant gratification—wanting what you want and wanting it now. Exercise, for example, gets quickly set aside when you feel short on time and the instant results of a healthy lifestyle aren't right in front of you. The same happens even more with prayer. But that's the opposite of what you should do.

Dr. Caroline Leaf concludes that toxic emotions experienced by this "busy-rush syndrome" actually cause disruptions to the autonomic nervous system and lead to a myriad of health problems like coronary disease and arrhythmia (having an erratic heart rhythm). That's why Fortune 500 CEOs are three times more likely than others to exercise, because they know that it reduces stress and boosts their energy. Challenge your excuses for what you do or don't prioritize. Here's how one mother defined the word *excuse:* "Son, an excuse is nothing but a lie stuffed inside the skin of a reason."

Plans and schedules are important, but you shouldn't be chained to them. Opportunities are seldom scheduled. So leave some space in your agenda to allow God to interrupt your plans. It can be disconcerting to not have every minute of the day consumed with doing. Henri Nouwen said, "We are afraid of emptiness...but God wants to dwell in our emptiness."[3] If you believe that the all-powerful God is present with you everywhere you are and is ready to speak and act on your behalf, then give your mind the opportunity to talk to Him and invite Him into your situation.

The highest priority on your list must always be staying connected to the Presence of God and listening to His still, small voice. It's hard to take the deluge of events that come rushing in every day and decide what you will make a priority. Dallas Willard says that the world shouts and God whispers. Life is an adventure, but too much on your mind and too many irons in the fire can eventually put out the fire. Prioritize!

> The key is not to prioritize what's on your schedule, but to schedule your priorities. —Stephen Covey

You don't hear much about the characteristic of "temperance" these days. *Temperance* is sort of an old-fashioned word that is defined as "moderation in action, thought, or feeling: restraint—habitual moderation in the indulgence of the appetites or passions."[4]

CHARACTERISTIC 34: TEMPERANCE

We have actually spoken a great deal about taming the appetites as a central purpose for this *40 Day Soul Fast*—making *"no provision for [indulging] the flesh"* (Rom. 13:14 AMP) and abstaining *"from fleshly lusts, which war against the soul"* (1 Pet. 2:11 KJV).

Temperance is one of the seven attributes we are told to *"add to our faith"* by Peter.

> *Add to your faith virtue; and to virtue knowledge; and to knowledge temperance; and to temperance patience; and to patience godliness; and to godliness brotherly kindness; and to brotherly kindness charity* (2 Peter 1:5-7 KJV).

Temperance is one of the nine fruits of the Spirit Paul wrote to the Galatians about: *"The fruit of the Spirit is love, joy, peace, longsuffering, gentleness, goodness, faith, meekness, temperance"* (Gal. 5:22-23 KJV). Paul wrote Titus to tell people to live *"lives of temperance, dignity, and wisdom, into healthy faith, love, and endurance"* (Titus 2:1).

The wisdom of the Bible tells us to do all things in moderation and to *"let your moderation be known unto all men"* (Phil. 4:5 KJV). Proverbs states that, *"Moderation is better than muscle, self-control better than political power"* (Prov. 16:32). Great leaders have fallen because of their lack of self-control. Accomplished men and women of God have compromised their faith and ministry simply because they were unable to exercise restraint.

- Examine your life. Where might the enemy have a foothold in the door of your soul, causing you to stumble in some area?

- What can you do to "clean house" in order make sure you are *"temperate in all things?"* What might your little "excesses" say to others about you?

Don't use your lack of moderation or self-restraint in some area as a hiding place from your true self—your better self. While some hide in entertainment, others hide in overeating, even others in sports or socializing. Take time to simply "be still" and exercise temperance.

Being forced to work, and forced to do your best, will breed in you temperance and self-control, diligence and strength of will, cheerfulness and contentment, and a hundred virtues which the idle will never know. —Charles Kingsley

There are no better cosmetics than a severe temperance and purity, modesty and humility, a gracious temper and calmness of spirit; and there is no true beauty without the signatures of these graces in the very countenance. —Arthur Helps

Yes, in the past you lived the way the world lives, following the ruler of the evil powers that are above the earth. That same spirit is now working in those who refuse to obey God. In the past all of us lived like them, trying to please our sinful selves and doing all the things our bodies and minds wanted (Ephesians 2:2-3 NCV).

Day Thirty-five

Willing

I am not bound to win, but I am bound to be true.
I am not bound to succeed, but I am bound to live
up to what light I have. —Abraham Lincoln

In 1940, the newspaper headlines were filled with the story of an undersized, knobby-kneed horse by the name of Seabiscuit who had become a champion of hope during the Great Depression. Early in his life he was known for sleeping and eating for long periods of time and was even the butt of stable jokes. Eventually the owners sold the horse, thinking it had no great potential. But a wise handler took the castaway and was able to slowly draw out the strength of body and the unbeatable spirit within. Seabiscuit, the same horse that most people judged as ordinary at best, went on to win the horse of the year and became horseracing's all-time leading money winner. *The Saturday Evening Post* attributed it to the fact that he "came from nothing on his own courage and will to win."

What you do in this life is in direct proportion to your courage and ability *to will*, to set your eyes on a goal and head toward it. Unlike crossing the finish line first in a horserace, winning or being successful as a disciple of Christ is a great deal more difficult to define. Jesus provided His own mission statement this way:

I came down from heaven not to follow My own whim but to accomplish the will of the One who sent Me. This, in a

> *nutshell, is that will: that everything handed over to Me by the Father be completed—not a single detail missed—and at the wrap-up of time I have everything and everyone put together, upright and whole* (John 6:38-39).

Being *willing* is about opening yourself up to whatever God has in store for you. It means to run headlong into your destiny, totally abandoned to something you can't see with your natural eyes so you must trust in the One who can get you there. That's the key found in Jesus' personal mission: He is charged with the task of seeing that you become upright and whole, and He promises not to miss a detail. That is what He came to do in your life. It does require, however, for you to will it.

In this success-driven society we find ourselves in, it is odd to think that the bottom line might not be what we expect it is—success might not look like we think it does. It's not that success isn't part of God's will for you; it is that success is a byproduct of what God wills for you. You could not possibly think up what God wants for you—your dreams would be too small. What you can control and make happen doesn't come close to what God has in mind. True success requires you to be willing to let go as you let God work out His will through you. In the *Renovare Spiritual Formation Bible,* Eugene Peterson writes:

> The mystery...is not the mystery of darkness that must be dispelled, but the mystery of light that may be entered. God and His operations cannot be reduced to what we are capable of explaining and then reproducing. It takes considerable humility to embrace this mystery, for in the presence of mystery

we are not in a position to control anything, predict outcomes, manage people, or pose as authorities.[1]

The apostle Paul is held up as a giant of the faith, following Jesus all over the known world, facing all kinds of hardships, and eventually laying down his life for Him. But even he knew that he played only a bit part in the great story God is still writing today. He set his will to the will of the Father and never looked back, trusting that it wasn't all up to him—knowing that only God knew the destiny of every believer. He said this in Acts 20 as he left his work "unfinished" by worldly standards, but not by God's:

> *I've done my best for you, given you my all, held back nothing of God's will for you. Now it's up to you.... Now I am turning you over to God, our marvelous God whose gracious Word can make you into what He wants you to be and give you everything you could possible need* (Acts 20:27-28,32).

The highest reward for man's toil is not what he gets for it, but what he becomes by it. —John Ruskin

This week we are talking about what I call "the power of doing." What you *do* can be as toxic to your soul as what you *think* or *say*—your actions have as much power to pollute or purify as your thoughts and words.

CHARACTERISTIC 35: MORALITY

This is the foundation of "God's chosen fast" described in Isaiah 58:

This is the kind of fasting I want: Free those who are wrongly imprisoned; lighten the burden of those who work for you. Let the oppressed go free, and remove the chains that bind people. Share your food with the hungry, and give shelter to the homeless. Give clothes to those who need them, and do not hide from relatives who need your help (Isaiah 58:6-7 NLT).

God's chosen fast is a call to do what is right—it is a call to *"do justly, and to love kindness and mercy"* (Mic. 6:8 AMP). It's a call to honor God by living ethical and moral lives.

Morality simply means virtuous conduct—"behavior or qualities judged to be good"—based on a set of principles concerning the distinction between right and wrong or good and bad behavior. It's doing things God's way.

After posing this question to the Galatians: *"What happens when we live God's way?"* Paul gave the answer: *"He brings gifts into our lives, much the same way that fruit appears in an orchard— things like affection for others, exuberance about life, serenity."* Most importantly, Paul said, *"We develop a willingness to stick with things,"* which develops in us *"a sense of compassion...and a conviction that a basic holiness permeates things and people."* Not only that, Paul adds, *"We find ourselves involved in loyal commitments, not needing to force our way in life, able to marshal and direct our energies wisely"* (Gal. 5:22-23).

When you find yourself having difficulty "directing your energies wisely," check to make sure you're doing whatever you do "God's way" and not your own way.

- Stop and reflect for a few moments on the verse below. Are any of the indicators listed here of "what happens when you do things your own way" present in your life?

It is obvious what kind of life develops out of trying to get your own way all the time...a stinking accumulation of mental and emotional garbage; frenzied and joyless grabs for happiness...paranoid loneliness; cutthroat competition; all-consuming-yet-never-satisfied wants; a brutal temper; an impotence to love or be loved; divided homes and divided lives; small-minded and lopsided pursuits; the vicious habit of depersonalizing everyone into a rival; uncontrolled and uncontrollable addictions (Galatians 5:19-21).

Learning to harness the power of holiness by doing things God's way—by developing strong moral character—will bring you true success and freedom.

I never did, or countenanced, in public life, a single act inconsistent with the strictest good faith; having never believed there was one code of morality for a public, and another for a private man. —Thomas Jefferson

Since this is the kind of life we have chosen, the life of the Spirit, let us make sure that we do not just hold it as an idea in our heads or a sentiment in our hearts, but work out its implications in every detail of our lives (Galatians 5:25-26).

Week Eight

Sealing the Healing: The Cleansing Power of Love

Day Thirty-six

Dancing

> As long as we approach another person from our loneliness, no mature human relationship can develop. Clinging to one another in loneliness is suffocating and eventually becomes destructive. For love to be possible we need the courage to create space between us and to trust that this space allows us to dance together. —Henri Nouwen[1]

Walking with Jesus in this life has several elements in common with pair figure skating in the Olympics. It is a beautiful sight to watch a young couple move together in unison as they dance in rhythm across the ice. The woman is lifted, whirled, and thrown by the gifted and able-bodied partner that she trusts completely. Did you ever stop to think about which one to watch—him or her? Not likely if their performance is flawless—they are seen as one, neither of them standing out.

In the dance of life, it is sometimes confusing to understand what is your part and what is God's and which is more important. Of course, you naturally think it is God—He is the one who leads and carries and spins us around—but without you, there wouldn't be much to see. In ballroom dancing, all eyes are usually on the woman who is framed and supported by her partner. Without her partner, however, there would be no performance. It takes both the lead and the one being led to complete the dance.

You might think to yourself, "Certainly God can bring love and justice to the world without me." Certainly He could. Yet for whatever reason, God has chosen to work through people from the beginning of time. He has designed your part to be inseparably linked together with His part, much like a pair of dancers or figure skaters. When it comes to loving the world, God intends to do it through you as you trust Him to be your partner in the dance.

John wrote:

> *The way we know we've been transferred from death to life is that we love our brothers and sisters. Anyone who doesn't love is as good as dead* (1 John 3:14).

Love is more than doing good toward another, although it does result in that. Paul, the writer of the famous love chapter, First Corinthians 13, understood that even if you give all that you have away—including your own body to be burned—and don't do it out of love, it is meaningless. It is only possible for you to love at all because of God's love in you. If you're not motivated by the love of God flowing through you, you will seek something for yourself—praise, recognition, favor, or a sense of being loved in return. Nothing but God's love—*agape* love—is authentic love.

John Eldridge states, "You cannot love another while you remain a captive."[2] Your heart must be set free in order to love without asking anything in return. Don't try to short-cut the process by simply acting lovingly. It is my hope that the work you've been doing these past seven weeks has liberated your heart to more fully receive—and give—love. A soul healed and made whole—set free from the tyranny of self (see 1 Pet. 4:1)—is critical to restructuring the world for good through love.

God's plan for loving the world—and the consequences for not doing your part—are found in First John 3:

If you see some brother or sister in need and have the means to do something about it but turn a cold shoulder and do nothing, what happens to God's love? It disappears. And you made it disappear (1 John 3:17).

God not only gives you eyes to see the need, but also provides the means for you to do something about it; your part is to do it.

When you prohibit the love of God moving through you, not only is love lost for the intended person, but you are "as good as dead." That means that your soul and body become governed by earthly passions and desires again, diminishing your true self. You've worked too hard to let that happen!

The great news is that when your heart and soul experience the love of God and you pass that on to others, your body and mind are actually changed as your heart speeds up its communication with the mind and body and it pulls every system into rhythm with it. Maybe that is what the writer of Acts 13:22 had in mind, writing about David: *"He's a man whose heart beats to My heart, a man who will do what I tell him."* Talk about rhythm and dance! Get in step with God and go love the world!

You will find as you look back upon your life that the moments when you have really lived, are the moments when you have done things in a spirit of love. —Henry Drummond

Yesterday we talked about the characteristic of morality and why it is so important in our journey toward authenticity.

Justice, like morality, has to do with our actions and behaviors. Justice, however, takes us one step further in that it has more to do with how we treat other people than it does following a set of principles regarding how we conduct our personal lives. Justice is about what we do on behalf of others.

CHARACTERISTIC 36: JUSTICE

A person who has a sense of justice treats others with fairness, is respectful of the rights and needs of others, and is non-partial when it comes to showing kindness and mercy. This person will feel compelled to intercede on behalf of those less fortunate or speak up on behalf of someone who is being treated unfairly.

We can work on behalf of social justice, strive for political justice, serve on behalf of those seeking legal justice, or simply "do justly" as God told us to do through the prophet Micah:

> *The Lord has told you, human, what is good; He has told you what He wants from you: to do what is right to other people, love being kind to others, and live humbly, obeying your God* (Micah 6:8 NCV).

Throughout the Bible we see that justice and mercy go hand in hand. Without mercy, there would be no motivation for justice. Justice is more than legalism; it is active compassion that drives us to stand up for the greater good—to oppose evil, as this newspaper tagline from before the turn of the 19th century states: "Dedicated in perpetuity to the service of the people, that no good cause shall lack a champion and that evil shall not thrive unopposed."[3]

304

We should not get so preoccupied with our own lives that we neglect our duty to pursue justice on behalf of all. Jesus admonished those who tithed, yet *"neglected the weightier matters of the law: justice and mercy and faith"* (Matt. 23:23 NKJV).

- How might you be neglecting the weightier matters of justice and mercy?

- What can you begin doing today to "serve people" and make sure evil does not thrive unopposed?

Never forget that, *"The Lord blesses the home of the just"* (Prov. 3:33)—those willing to stand in the gap. Go back to Isaiah 58:6-8. May you be found among those who do justice and love mercy, imitating and *"obeying your God"* (Mic. 6:8 NCV).

Without justice and love, peace will always be the great illusion. —Archbishop Helder Pessoa Camara

For unto us a Child is born, unto us a Son is given; and the government will be upon His shoulder. And His name will be called Wonderful, Counselor, Mighty God, Everlasting Father, Prince of Peace. Of the increase of His government and peace there will be no end, upon the throne of David and over His kingdom, to order it and establish it with judgment and justice from that time forward, even forever. The zeal of the Lord of hosts will perform this (Isaiah 9:6-7 NKJV).

Day Thirty-seven

Accepting

How far you go in life depends on your being tender with the young, compassionate with the aged, sympathetic with the striving, and tolerant of the weak and strong. Because someday in your life you will have been all of these. —George Washington Carver

Marginalized people continuously show up in the stories of Jesus—prostitutes, tax collectors, soldiers, criminals, poor people, sick people, old people, and children. It would be easy to see the mission of Jesus as a fixer of what's broken. That's understandably what most people feel inclined to do when they encounter chaos in the lives of others—to fix them. But what determines brokenness? Jesus saw people so differently than the world sees them, accepting and loving them where they were and tolerating their weaknesses even as He loved them into more than they could imagine or ask.

Duane Elmer, in his book *Cross-Cultural Servanthood*, tells the parable of a monkey who sees a fish swimming against the current of a stream. Assuming the fish is struggling to survive, the monkey plucks the fish out of the stream and places it on dry ground with him. At first, the fish flops around, excited to have been saved—at least that's what the monkey thinks. Even when the fish stops moving, the monkey feels satisfied, believing that the fish is resting contentedly. But of course, the fish is dead![1]

The monkey saw a creature "broken" and decided that the "fix" was to give the fish what the monkey thought he would need. Isn't that typical of how people relate to differences? Rather than asking if they even want help, the world whips out the hammers, saws, and nails and begins a makeover project. No matter how badly you want it, people don't fix people. To live out your destiny and impact the world on God's behalf you must not only accept other people where they are, but be grateful God has caused you to cross paths. What do they have to teach you?

C.S. Lewis tells the story of lecturing to a group of people shortly after World War II. He was interrupted by an old soldier who said that he had no use for Lewis' dogmas and formulas about God, having felt God for himself while out in the desert alone one night. Words could not begin to describe what he had experienced. Lewis agreed that what the man was expressing was a little like a map being compared to the Atlantic Ocean. A piece of paper could not replace the real waves of the sea. But, it could do something that this man's experience could not:

> The map is based on what hundreds and thousands
> of people have found out by sailing the real Atlantic.
> In that way it has behind it masses of experience just
> as real as the one you could have from the beach;
> only, while yours would be a single isolated glimpse,
> the map fits all those different experiences together.[2]

God is much bigger than your view of Him, and He will use all kinds of people—especially those on the margins—to broaden your understanding of that. Your task is to love and accept them where they are. Human beings will never be able to fully "map" out God, but it will take the experiences of each one to even get a small glimpse.

> I am not called to judge my neighbor, but to serve them as best I can by the light I have, humbly and patiently, with the strength I have and the strength God supplies. The best gift I can give them is always the character and power of Christ in me and in others who really trust Him. If we must part at some point in where we spend eternity, I shall love them none the less for it. —Dallas Willard[3]

Yesterday we talked about how justice and mercy go hand in hand. Today I want to talk to you about tolerance—because tolerance is what gives you the capacity to be merciful.

CHARACTERISTIC 37: TOLERANCE

Tolerance is the ability to accept the differences of others. It enables you to show patience, compassion, and charity.

Tolerance is not about condoning undermining and evil behavior, immoral lifestyles, or unethical dealings, but is about the ability and capacity to embrace the differences in others as well as their right to choose their destiny, beliefs and convictions. It is understanding that God has given each one of us the freedom of choice and each one of us must choose the path we take in life. God gives all of us the freedom of choice.

The Bible talks about the importance of a leader being able to show tolerance. Hebrews talks about the high priest who *"is able to deal gently with ignorant and wayward people because he himself is subject to the same weaknesses"* (Heb. 5:2 NLT).

God Himself is tolerant beyond what most of us are capable of understanding. In his letter to the Romans, Paul chided:

> *Do you have contempt for the riches of God's generosity, tolerance, and patience? Don't you realize that God's kindness is supposed to lead you to change your heart and life?* (Romans 2:4 CEB)

Our own tolerance toward others can be used as a mechanism to bring them to repentance and the knowledge of God. First Peter 3 talks about wives winning their husbands over not by being judgmental, but by being tolerant.

Proverbs tells us that it is *"By long forbearance and calmness of spirit a judge or ruler is persuaded, and soft speech breaks down the most bonelike resistance"* (Prov. 25:15 AMP). Conversely, Proverbs also states that, *"He who is slow to anger has great understanding, but he who is hasty of spirit exposes and exalts his folly"* (Prov. 14:29 AMP).

Tolerance can also be defined as "the power or capacity of an organism to tolerate unfavorable environmental conditions." Imagine what that kind of power could do for you.

- How would you rate your capacity to tolerate unfavorable conditions? What does this say about your own degree of personal empowerment?

- How are you harnessing the power of tolerance to change the hearts and lives of those around you? In what small way might you show a little more tolerance?

Remember, *"He who is slow to anger is better than the mighty, he who rules his [own] spirit than he who takes a city"* (Prov. 16:32 AMP).

Don't underestimate the power of tolerance to change hearts and circumstances. When you exercise tolerance, you are exercising your faith in the power of God's goodness to soften hearts and His grace to overpower evil.

When you find peace within yourself, you become the kind of person who can live at peace with others.
—Mildred Lisette Norman

Through His faithfulness, God displayed Jesus as the place of sacrifice where mercy is found by means of His blood. He did this to demonstrate His righteousness in passing over sins that happened before, during the time of God's patient tolerance. He also did this to demonstrate that He is righteous in the present time, and to treat the one who has faith in Jesus as righteous (Romans 3:25-26 CEB).

Day Thirty-eight

Standing

Give me a lever long enough and a fulcrum on which to place it, and I shall move the world.
—Archimedes

Although he didn't say it in this quote, Archimedes no doubt assumed there would be ground on which to place his fulcrum. God began providing a place for you to stand before the world began. Genesis says that God separated the waters above and the waters below and created the land—a firm place for your feet to stand and move the world with love. God told Joshua to walk the land and that everywhere he placed his foot He would give it to him (see Josh. 1:3). David's mighty men each had a field in which to take a stand and fight for their king. Where is your field, your place to stand and love the world?

It's so easy to assume that where you are now isn't where you are supposed to be, or is at least not the place of your destiny. It must surely be a different time and place, right? "How could God ever do amazing things in this place?" you might ask. Stranger things have happened. Consider Saul out looking for a lost donkey and coming home anointed as king. Then there was David who took a boxed lunch to his brothers and he ended up slaying a giant named Goliath. Moses was drafted to lead a million people out of Egypt while tending sheep on the backside of the desert. Henri Nouwen says it is quite possible that your destiny begins right where you are: "Let's be patient and trust that the treasure we look for is hidden in the ground on which we stand."[1]

It is interesting that God only imposed one limitation on Adam and Eve. He gave them only one thing they were not to do—eat from the Tree of the Knowledge of Good and Evil. Otherwise, they were free to make choices and expand their kingdom as far as their abilities would allow. How you choose to extend God's Kingdom and distribute His power and love to the world is wide open and full of freedom. You are only restricted by ethics and moral law.

To love means to create a place for someone else to also be able to stand, to make their own way, and choose for themselves. Dallas Willard proposes that, "to make a place for another is one of the most life-giving and life-receiving things a human being can do."[2] This is a beautiful statement summarizing a noble truth. You give life and receive it back when you create a place for another.

Dennis Bakke, previous owner of one of the largest power companies in the world, writes in his book, *Joy at Work,* that he restricted himself as the head of the company in regard to decision-making so that others could decide, even in strategic situations. Bakke wanted every person to experience the joy of choice—to be part of making something happen and be responsible for the results. He created a place to stand for employees in developing countries who had never known the feeling of choosing for themselves—something Bakke considers part of being made in the image of God.

Where you take your stand and live out your destiny is determined by who God has called you to be. A "king-and-a-priest" is called to a group of people, not a project, and certainly not the whole world. You will burn yourself out quickly if you try to be everything to everybody. Your thoughts and energy will be diluted.

Paul tells the Colossians in chapter 3 to plant their feet firmly on the ground where they were and hold their heads up high. That's good advice for you too. Stand firm!

> When you take a stand out of deep conviction, people know. They may not even agree, but they ask, "Do I want someone who is willing to take a hard stand and someone I can trust to do that when the chips are down?" They want that. —Barbara Boxer

As we wind down our *40 Day Soul Fast*, we are talking about the importance of "being" and "doing"—the impact our behaviors and actions have on the world around us—and how that in turn is reflected back to us in the way we experience life.

CHARACTERISTIC 38: ETHICS

We began this journey toward authenticity talking about the inner life of the soul. As we have progressed through the 40 days, we have moved out from our own internal awareness of the life of our souls to an understanding of the power of our thoughts, our identity, and our words. This week, we are talking about how all of these elements affect how we relate to others. We are focusing on the principles outlined in Isaiah 58, "God's Chosen Fast," because here we are told that God will honor us only to the extent we honor other people.

We have talked about the importance of demonstrating morality, justice, and tolerance. As we grow toward authenticity, our lives become more and more transparent, requiring us to rise to an ever-higher standard of accountability. Becoming more authentic, more genuine, more "real" requires a deeper sense of truthfulness, honesty, and honor. Our truest intentions are revealed. Our integrity is tested. Our credibility is established.

This is what the concept of *ethics* represents: That which is motivated by pure, noble, and honorable intentions—an uprightness in choices, values, business dealings, and professional aspirations. What you choose to do with your money, how you handle it—whether generously or selfishly—is a good indication of personal ethics.

Your sense of ethics will require you to take a stand. As it says in Isaiah, *"If you don't take your stand in faith, you won't have a leg to stand on"* (Isa. 7:7); and in Galatians, *"Take your stand! Never again let anyone put a harness of slavery on you"* (Gal. 5:1); and in Ephesians, *"Take your stand against the devil's schemes"* (Eph. 6:11 NIV).

Stand up for what you believe in. Those whose hearts are upright before God will be required to stand up on behalf of those who can't stand up for themselves—to stand up for the oppressed—to stand up against evil! Let your life make a statement by taking a stand.

Ethics is a call to action! What are you doing to "show forth" the goodness of God? *"Let him by his noble living show forth his [good] works"* (James 3:13 AMP).

- In bringing something to your attention, could God be requiring you to take a stand?

Bestselling author, Gary Zukav, reminds us that, "You are only as powerful as that for which you stand."

I leave you today with this famous prayer by the Scottish-American preacher, Peter Marshall: "Give to us clear vision that we may know where to stand and what to stand for—because unless we stand for something, we shall fall for anything."

The ultimate measure of a man is not where he stands in moments of comfort and convenience, but where he stands at times of challenge and controversy. —Martin Luther King Jr.

When you're kind to others, you help yourself; when you're cruel to others, you hurt yourself. Bad work gets paid with a bad check; good work gets solid pay. Take your stand with God's loyal community and live, or chase after phantoms of evil and die. God can't stand deceivers, but oh how He relishes integrity (Proverbs 11:17-20).

Day Thirty-nine

Uniting

If I have been able to see further than others, it is because I stood on the shoulders of giants. —Sir Isaac Newton

On September 11, 2001, researchers from New Zealand to Israel noted a statistical spike in the results posted from dozens of random number-generating computers for a project on global consciousness. *USA Today* published an article asking if the events of that day had refocused "an interconnected web of global consciousness." Researchers themselves don't want to talk about it for fear that focusing the minds of masses of people around the globe on the project will skew their tests. However, it does make you wonder, doesn't it?

Are we all connected in some unconscious way? Only God knows the answer for sure, but Scripture does speak often of the common life that we live. C.S. Lewis, in *Mere Christianity*, says this about the connectedness of humans:

But human beings are not (all separate). They look separate because you see them walking about separately. But then, we are so made that we can see only the present moment. If we could see the past, then of course it would look different. For there was a time when every man was part of his mother, and (earlier still) part of his father as well: and when they were part of his grandparents. If you could see humanity spread out in time, as God sees it, it would not look like a lot of separate things dotted about. It would look like one single growing thing—rather like a very complicated tree. Every individual would appear connected with every other.[1]

How does knowing that you are connected in some way to others affect how you love them? It certainly gives a whole new meaning to Jesus' command to "love your neighbor as yourself"—or His prayer in John 17 that those following Him would all be one. According to John, Jesus died *"for the purpose of uniting into one body the children of God"* (John 11:52 AMP).

The metaphor of the body pictured in Romans 12 lays out the idea of interconnectedness in a way that is easily understood by all, saying in verse 5 that we are members one of another. Paul explained another time to the Corinthians that when he suffered on their behalf, it worked toward their good, and when *"we are treated well, given a helping hand and encouraging word, that also works to your benefit, spurring you on, face forward, unflinching"* (2 Cor. 1:6). Even the act of giving links people together. Paul wrote to the Philippians about their gift to him saying, *"Not that I seek the gift itself, but I seek for the profit which increases to your account"* (Phil. 4:17 NASB).

Whether you love people by giving financially, by sharing your wisdom and knowledge, or by exercising your gifts and talents, your life is directly united to others and is interdependent on their reciprocating acts of love toward you. Scripture outlines the joining of your life with others with statements like: "Be at peace with one another;" "love one another;" "be devoted to one another;" "accept one another;" "serve one another;" "bear one another's burdens;" "be kind to one another;" "prefer one another." You get the idea.

Mark Twain once said: "To get the full value of joy you must have someone to divide it with." Love others lavishly—because in truth, you are showering love on yourself!

> Self-actualizing people have a deep feeling of identification, sympathy, and affection for human beings in general. They feel kinship and connection, as if all people were members of a single family. —Abraham Maslow

Yesterday we talked about ethics and taking a stand on behalf of others—today we will talk about why this is so important.

CHARACTERISTIC 39: INTERDEPENDENCE

Interestingly, the more authentic we become, the more interdependent we will be. As the dividing walls and facades come down, we learn to trust in and rely on one another—we realize we need each other to complete one another.

As we grow into our truest selves, we learn where we fit into the whole—and that our wholeness comes from being "jointly fit together in love" as we are told in Ephesians:

> *As each part does its own special work, it helps the other parts grow, so that the whole body is healthy and growing and full of love* (Ephesians 4:16 NLT).

This is a beautiful illustration of interdependence. This kind of "oneness" is central to Christ's entire mission on the Earth. It is worth reiterating:

It was also Christ's purpose to...make them into one body, and to bring them back to God. Christ did all this with His death on the cross (Ephesians 2:16 NCV).

Throughout the New Testament, we are told over and over that in Christ, we are one body. We are told to be of one mind, one heart, one spirit, because we belong to each other:

In the same way, we are many, but in Christ we are all one body. Each one is a part of that body, and each part belongs to all the other parts (Romans 12:5 NCV).

It is for this reason that all of the characteristics of an authentic person are so important—being honest, forthright, upright, and, as Paul told the Ephesians:

rejecting all falsity and being done now with it, let everyone express the truth with his neighbor, for we are all parts of one body and members one of another (Ephesians 4:25 AMP).

Most importantly, interdependence is what allows you to say, *"It is no longer I who live, but Christ lives in me"* (Gal. 2:20 NLT).

- How deep is your sense of interdependence?

Are you able to say as Paul did, *"Everyone I meet—it matters little whether they're mannered or rude, smart or simple—deepens my sense of interdependence and obligation"* (Rom. 1:13)?

I can never be what I ought to be until you are what you ought to be. This is the way our world is made. No individual or nation can stand out boasting of being independent. We are interdependent. —Martin Luther King, Jr.

You can easily enough see how this kind of thing works by looking no further than your own body. Your body has many parts—limbs, organs, cells—but no matter how many parts you can name, you're still one body. It's exactly the same with Christ. By means of His one Spirit, we all said good-bye to our partial and piecemeal lives. We each used to independently call our own shots, but then we entered into a large and integrated life in which He has the final say in everything (1 Corinthians 12:12).

Day Forty

Telling

When the lessons of the past are offered without the stories that led to them, it is difficult, if not impossible, for us to learn from the experience of others.... Stories nourish our soul as well as our intellect. —Richard Stone[1]

Telling stories with a community of believers is an important part of growing into maturity in the Christian life. Eugene Peterson says, "I am not myself by myself."[2] There are those who are content to keep the past in a treasure chest, secretly opening it occasionally to savor the memories—reading the maps, looking at the photographs, and picturing again the great escapades and accomplishments of yesterday. Some people never venture out themselves at all, but live their lives through the stories of others. Neither of those are the kind of life that God has for you! But becoming a storyteller is.

In Matthew 13, Jesus spends the afternoon telling stories to the people, fulfilling a prophecy that said: *"I will open My mouth and tell stories; I will bring out into the open things hidden since the world's first day"* (Matt. 13:35). When asked by some of His disciples why He spent so much time telling stories, He replied, *"I tell stories: to create readiness, to nudge people toward receptive insight"* (Matt. 13:13). In other words, He was preparing the soil for the seed, a topic He expanded upon throughout the day in order to help them understand what the Kingdom of God is like and how they play a part in it.

One of those stories said that God's Kingdom is like a farmer who sowed *"pure seed."* Jesus, when asked, explained that He Himself is the farmer and that the seeds are the believers—subjects of the Kingdom. In another narrative that day He said that God's Kingdom is like a pine nut that a farmer plants. *"It is quite small as seeds go, but in the course of years it grows into a huge pine tree, and eagles build nests in it"* (Matt. 13:32). Then He shares with the listeners that the Kingdom of God is like a treasure hidden in a field, accidently found by a "trespasser" who sells everything to buy that field.

Stories force the listeners to connect their lives with parts of the story being told. Your mind cannot help but offer up connections buried like treasure within you when you encounter the words of Jesus and others. You are the seed planted by Jesus in a field—a treasure for others to find. You are the pine nut who starts out full of potential seen only by the Creator God and yet, nurtured by His ways, grows into a huge tree of life in which others can find a secure place to birth and foster their young dreams.

But who is the "trespasser" who stumbles "accidently" on the treasure? And what is the treasure? The discoverer is for sure not one who has any right to claim it, and yet he has been mysteriously guided to cross paths with it. Psalm 19 reveals that God's Word directs you to buried treasure, and although you have no right to it by any human law, by the blood of Jesus Christ you may give up everything to have it. The trespasser might be the one Jesus refers to that day as seeking and ready to receive: *"Whenever someone has a ready heart for this* [how the Kingdom of God operates] *the insights and understandings flow freely"* (Matt. 13:11-15).

Then the understanding of the treasure becomes clearer. It contains the resources and insights of those like you who allow themselves to be transformed by the "ways-that-are-higher-than-your-ways." Then these are told as stories to others in a way that prepares the soil of their hearts to receive. As you become your true self and tell your story to others, you become part of a cloud of witnesses, a city set on a hill whose light shines brightly and who collectively witness to the love of God for the world! So let your light shine!

> Stories are the creative conversion of life itself into a more powerful, clearer, more meaningful experience. They are the currency of human contact.
> —Robert McKee

Congratulations! Here we are on the very last day of *The 40 Day Soul Fast!* I commend you on completing the journey and pray that you are living more authentically as a result.

CHARACTERISTIC 40: COMMUNITY

Connection, collaboration, communication, acceptance, compassion, respect, support, safety, shared values, inclusion, kindness, tolerance, understanding, and inspiration are a few words that come to mind when I think of community. As we bring our journey together to a close, I want to talk to you about what I believe is the nearest and dearest thing to God's heart. Building community is not a political or economic process, but purely spiritual and relational. It is ultimately about corporate destiny—our destiny as a collaborative entity. It is about living and working together so that we can make this world a better place for everyone. When you build community, there is no big "I" and little "you," but simply "we" and "us."

Jesus said, *"Your love for one another will prove to the world that you are My disciples"* (John 13:35 NLT). Paul prayed, *"May the Lord make your love for one another and for all people grow and overflow, just as our love for you overflows"* (1 Thess. 3:12 NLT), and added, *"We can't help but thank God for you, because your faith is flourishing and your love for one another is growing"* (2 Thess. 1:3 NLT). Peter wrote, *"Above all things have intense and unfailing love for one another, for love covers a multitude of sins [forgives and disregards the offenses of others]"* (1 Pet. 4:8 AMP).

This is what living in community is all about. It's God's best will for His people. It's what floods the world with light and turns it upside right.

Community requires that we walk in love with one another as we each strive to become our best and most authentic selves. It calls us to represent Christ, to be walking epistles— the word made flesh, the hope of glory that Christ, alive in you, is to a dark and dying world.

Gandhi said, "Be the change you want to see." I'm challenging you to "be the light you want to see." As Marianne Williamson so famously said, "And as we let our own light shine, we unconsciously give other people permission to do the same. As we are liberated from our own fear, our presence automatically liberates others."

- From this day forward, how will you shine a little brighter? Describe what that might look like and the affect it could have on the people you encounter.

- Change begins one thought, one soul, one life at a time. What is the one thought you can adopt that could change everything? What will be the new story you tell as a result?

- How can you start a conversation in your community—whether it is the workplace, church, neighborhood, or school—about living more authentically?

I encourage you to tell your story. Better yet, write a bigger story for yourself! As author Jean Houston has said, "If you keep telling the same sad small story, you will keep living the same sad small life." Become the author of your own enormous, authentic life.

Write me at drcindytrimm@trimminternational.com and let me know how living more authentically has made a difference not only within you, but also in the world around you! I believe that as each of us participates in the healing of our own souls, we are participating in the healing of our world. And together we can create a healing movement that will bring peace and prosperity to people everywhere.

> You must have control of the authorship of your own destiny. The pen that writes your life story must be held in your own hand. —Irene C. Kassorla

> *Beloved, I pray that you may prosper in all things and be in health, just as your soul prospers* (3 John 1:2 NKJV).

> Authentic Christians are persons who stand apart from others. Their character seems deeper, their ideas fresher, their spirit softer, their courage greater, their leadership stronger, their concerns wider, their compassion more genuine, and their convictions more concrete. —Bill Hybels

Appendix A

Empowering You for Life!

LOOKING FOR MORE?

Please visit me online at www.trimminternational.com for more tools and resources to nurture the life of your soul. If you want to take part in the Soul Fast Movement, please go to www.soulfast.com to find out how you can get involved, enroll in our ongoing programs, or participate in a guided, interactive 40 Day Soul Fast. Two times per year, I host an eight-week program when I personally coach you through each of the 40 Characteristics via my weekly empowerment broadcast, daily video blog, and downloadable phone app. There you also will find a *40 Day Soul Fast Cleansing Guide*, a free "Dynamic Life Questionnaire," an online community where you can always continue the conversation, as well as other soul-enhancing resources.

Let's do life together! Join with me as I endeavor to heal the world by healing the souls of individuals—empowering them to impact their communities and nations all across the globe. Every soul is significant and influences the world in countless ways. Never doubt that what you do *does* make a difference! You could be the answer someone else is looking for. Don't wait another day to step up to the plate—the world's next homerun could be depending on you to make the pitch. Pitch life. Pitch healing!

I value you and what you bring to the game. Let's make a difference and bring healing wherever we are. Let's make this life a winning proposition for all. For more about soul healing and empowerment, please visit me online. Join the soul healing movement or create your own. If you are interested in pioneering the unexplored frontiers of your own destiny, enroll in my signature *Executive Life Coaching* personal and professional achievement program, or register to attend a Trimm University intensive school of leadership, prayer, or ministry.

As always, I look forward to empowering you for life!

DR. CINDY TRIMM

Appendix B

More Empowerment Initiatives From

Dr. Cindy Trimm

Imagine The Possibilities!

Executive Life Coaching with Dr. Cindy Trimm is a 52-week success system for maximum personal and professional achievement. Join an elite group of protégés as Dr. Trimm takes you on an epic destiny-fulfilling journey.

From spearheading health outreaches in the inner city to building homes for orphans in southeast Asia, the Trimm Foundation strives to bring practical solutions and empowerment strategies to the places where hope and healing are needed most.

The Life Empowerment Program provides you with 365-days of life strategies designed to unlock your fullest potential. As your empowerment mentor, each day Dr. Cindy Trimm will share key principles and insights that will take you where you want to be a year from today. Imagine where your life could be this time next year! By making just a few adjustments, taking deliberate action with a little focused effort and conscious intention, you will make quantum progress. This is what this program is all about.

Receive a daily e-video teaching packed with practical life principles that will equip you to:

- Grow emotionally, professionally, relationally

- Discover and unlock the seed of greatness hidden with you

- Dramatically increase your ability to fulfill any goal or desire

- Add meaning to what you're doing

- Expand your influence with others

- Learn what it takes to win at life

- Put the "wow" back into daily living

Sign up today at www.yourlifeempowerment.com or call us at 866-444-7258.

Dr. Trimm is looking to heal communities by empowering individuals. Keep your eyes open for Dr. Trimm's upcoming book and worldwide campaign:

Heal Your Soul, Heal Our World.

Together, we can heal the world!

Visit www.TrimmInternational.com today!

SOON TO BE RELEASED:

Heal Your Soul, Heal Our World
Reclaim Your Soul
Reclaim Your Health
The Creed
The Quest
The Journey

OTHER RESOURCES FOR SPIRITUAL ENRICHMENT FROM DR. TRIMM INCLUDE:

The Prayer Warrior's Way

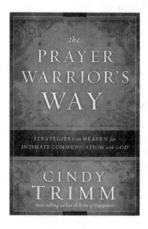

The Art of War for Spiritual Battle

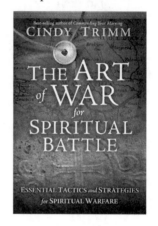

Commanding Your Morning

The Rules of Engagement

Endnotes

Preface

1. St. Augustine and Henry Chadwick, *Confessions* (Oxford, UK: Oxford University Press, 1992), 3.

2. Noelle Damico, "Fasting: A Spiritually and Socially Transforming Practice," Shenandoah Presbytery, 2, accessed July 30, 2011, http://www.shenpres.org/ HungerDocs/FastingSpirituallyTransforming.pdf.

Chapter One

1. Lemony Snicket. *A Series of Unfortunate Events: The Vile Village* (New York: Scholastic Inc, 2001), 1.

Chapter Two

1. *"And the Lord God formed man of the dust of the ground, and breathed into his nostrils the breath of life; and man became a living soul"* (Genesis 2:7 KJV).

2. *"Then God said, 'Let Us make man in Our image, according to Our likeness'"* (Genesis 1:26 NKJV).

3. See Matthew 28:19.

4. "[He has] *given us the Spirit in our hearts as a guarantee*" (2 Corinthians 1:22 NKJV).

5. *"God made great and marvelous promises, so that His nature would become part of us...That through these you may be partakers of the divine nature"* (2 Peter 1:4 CEV, NKJV).

6. *"You are an epistle of Christ"* (2 Corinthians 3:3 NKJV).

Chapter Three

1. Brown, Driver, and Briggs, *The Hebrew-English Lexicon* (Peabody, MA: Hendrickson Publishers, 1985), s.v. "Soul."

2. *"For there is a root of sinful self-interest in us that is at odds with a free spirit, just as the free spirit is incompatible with selfishness"* (Gal. 5:17). See also Galatians 5:19-21.

Chapter Four

1. Valerie Rickel, "Your Authentic Self," SoulfulLiving. com, May 2003, accessed August 02, 2011, http://www.soulfulliving.com/may03features.

2. Alex M. Wood et al., "The Authentic Personality: A Theoretical and Empirical Conceptualization and the Development of the Authenticity Scale," *Journal of Counseling Psychology* 55, no. 3 (2008): 385-399.

Chapter Five

1. Kay Nuyens, "Living an Authentic Life," SoulfulLiving.com, 2003, accessed August 02, 2011, http://www.soulfulliving.com/authentic_life.htm.

Day 1

1. *"You have been regenerated (born again), not from a mortal origin (seed, sperm), but from one that is immortal by the ever living and lasting Word of God"* (1 Pet. 1:23 AMP).

2. N.T. Wright, "After You Believe: Why Christian Character Matters," Center for Faith and Work, Redeemer Presbyterian Church, April 20, 2010, accessed August 02, 2011, http://www.faithandwork.org/ntwright.

3. Esther Hargis, "Being Church: Taking Risks," The First Baptist Church of Berkeley, California, May 18, 1997, accessed August 2, 2011, http://www.fbc-berkeley.org/risks.html.

Day 6

1. Eugene Peterson, *Christ Plays in Ten Thousand Places: A Conversation in Spiritual Theology* (Cambridge, U.K.: William B. Eerdmans Publishing Co., 2005), 337.

Day 7

1. Linda-Ann Steward, qtd. in Dutch Sheets, *Roll Away Your Stone: Living in the Power of the Risen Christ* (Minneapolis, MN: Bethany House, 2007), 83.

Day 9

1. Dallas Willard, *Hearing God* (Downers Grove, IL: InterVarsity Press, 1999), 204.

Day 11

1. Ibid., 193.

Day 13

1. *Wristcutters: A Love Story,* perf. Shannyn Sossamon and Tom Waits (Lionsgate, 2008), DVD.

Day 16

1. Willard, *Hearing God,* 77.

2. Ibid., 77.

Day 17

1. Ibid., 166.

2. Ibid., 147.

Day 18

1. Eugene H. Peterson, *Living The Message: Daily Help for Living the God-Centered Life* (New York, NY: HarperCollins, 1996), 147.

Day 20

1. Gary Sutliff, "Hyperspace and the Spiritual Realm at Louisiana Baptist University." (PhD diss., Louisiana Baptist University, n.d.), 3.

Day 22

1. Henri Nouwen, *Bread for the Journey: A Daybook of Wisdom and Faith* (New York, NY: HarperCollins Publishers, 1997), January 10.

2. Brennan Manning, *Abba's Child* (Colorado Springs, CO: NavPress, 2002), 24.

3. Kathleen Norris, *The Cloister Walk*, quoted in Dan B. Allender, *To Be Told* (Colorado Springs, CO: Water-Brook Press, 2005), 167.

Day 23

1. Allender, *To Be Told*, 69.

2. Albert L. Winseman, Donald O. Clifton, Curt Liesveld, *Living Your Strengths: Discover Your God-given Talents and Inspire Your Community* (New York, NY: Gallup Press, 2008), 2.

3. Ibid.

Day 24

1. Peter Heitt, Pastor of Lookout Community Church, printed transcript of sermon.

2. Margaret J. Wheatley, *Leadership and the New Science: Discovering Order in a Chaotic World* (San Francisco, CA: Berrett-Koehler Publishers, Inc., 2006), 35.

3. Parker Palmer, *Let Your Life Speak* (San Francisco, CA: Jossey-Bass, 2000), 34.

Day 25

1. Dr. Henry Cloud, *Integrity* (New York, NY: Harper-Collins Publishers, 2006), 206.

2. Ibid., 221.

Day 26

1. Eugene Peterson, *Eat This Book: A Conversation in the Art of Spiritual Reading* (Cambridge, U.K.: William B. Eerdmans Publishing Co., 2009), xi.

Day 27

1. Dr. Caroline Leaf, *Who Switched Off My Brain: Controlling Toxic Thoughts and Emotions* (South Africa: Switch Off Your Brain Ltd, 2007), 116.

Day 28

1. Henry Blackaby, *What the Spirit is Saying to the Churches* (Sisters, OR: Multnomah Publishers, 2003), 29.

Day 29

1. Leaf, *Who Switched Off My Brain, Controlling Toxic Thoughts and Emotions (South Africa: Switch Off Your Brain Ltd, 2007).*

2. Allan Hardman, *The Everything Toltec Wisdom Book: A Complete Guide to the Ancient Wisdoms* (Avon, MA: Adams Media, 2007), 123.

Day 30

1. Collins English Dictionary: Complete and Unabridged 10th Edition, s.v. "Compassion."

Day 34

1. John Eldredge, *Waking the Dead* (Nashville, TN: Thomas Nelson Publishers, 2003), 75.

2. David Allen, *Getting Things Done: The Art of Stress-Free Productivity* (New York, NY: Penguin Books, 2001), 7.

3. Nouwen, *Bread for the Journey*, February 28.

4. *Merriam-Webster*, s.v. "Temperance."

Day 35

1. Eugene Peterson, quoted in Richard Foster, editor, *The Renovare Spiritual Formation Bible* (San Francisco, CA: HarperCollins Publishers, 2005), 2045.

Day 36

1. Nouwen, *Bread for the Journey*, January 19.

2. Eldredge, *Waking the Dead*, 88.

3. *The Denver Post*, October 28, 1895.

Day 37

1. Duane Elmer, *Cross-Cultural Servanthood* (Downers Grove, IL: Intervarsity Press, 1999), 27-28.

2. C.S. Lewis, *Mere Christianity* (New York, NY: Collier Books, 1952), 119-120.

3. Dallas Willard, *Renovation of the Heart: Putting on the Character of Christ* (Colorado Springs, CO: NavPress, 2002), 255.

Day 38

1. Nouwen, *Bread for the Journey*, January 5.

2. Willard, *Renovation of the Heart*, 183.

Day 39

1. Lewis, *Mere Christianity*, 140-141.

Day 40

1. Marshall Goldsmith, Beverly Kaye, Ken Shelton, editors, *Learning Journeys: Lessons on Becoming Great Mentors and Leaders* (Palo Alto, CA: Davies-Black Publishing, 2000), 207.

2. Peterson, *Christ Plays in Ten Thousand Places*, 226.

About Dr. Cindy Trimm

A best-selling author, high impact teacher, and former senator, Dr. Trimm is a sought-after empowerment specialist, revolutionary thinker, and transformational leader. She has earned a distinguished reputation as a catalyst for change and voice of hope to the nations.

Listed among *Ebony* magazine's *Power 100* as the "top 100 doers and influencers in the world today," Dr. Trimm is a featured speaker on some of the world's largest platforms, a frequent guest on Christian broadcasting's most popular TV and radio shows, and continually tops the Black Christian News Network and Black Christian Book Company's National Bestsellers List.

Dr. Trimm combines her wealth of leadership expertise with her depth of spiritual understanding to reveal life-transforming messages that empower and inspire. Seasoned with humor, compassion, revelatory insight, and personal candor, Dr. Trimm opens minds and touches hearts with biblically-based principles of inner healing and personal empowerment.

Pulling on her background in government, education, psychology, and human development, Dr. Trimm translates hard-hitting spiritual insights into everyday language that empower individuals to transform their lives—helping change the path people take in search of meaning, dignity, purpose, and hope.

Discover Your AQ

What's Your Authenticity Quotient?
Be sure to visit www.soulfast.com to take the
free AQ Assessment and find out how authentically
you are living today!

Get the App

Share with your friends.
Track your progress
Keep up with your journal.
Change your life.

The 40 Day Soul Fast App

http://soulfast.destinyimage.com

IN THE RIGHT HANDS, THIS BOOK WILL CHANGE LIVES!

Most of the people who need this message will not be looking for this book. To change their lives, you need to put a copy of this book in their hands.

> *But others (seeds) fell into good ground, and brought forth fruit, some a hundred-fold, some sixty-fold, some thirty-fold* (Matthew 13:8).

Our ministry is constantly seeking methods to find the good ground, the people who need this anointed message to change their lives. Will you help us reach these people?

> *Remember this—a farmer who plants only a few seeds will get a small crop. But the one who plants generously will get a generous crop* (2 Corinthians 9:6).

EXTEND THIS MINISTRY BY SOWING
3 BOOKS, 5 BOOKS, 10 BOOKS, **OR MORE TODAY,**
AND BECOME A LIFE CHANGER!

Thank you,

Don Nori Sr., Founder
Destiny Image
Since 1982

DESTINY IMAGE PUBLISHERS, INC.

"Promoting Inspired Lives."

VISIT OUR NEW SITE HOME AT
WWW.DESTINYIMAGE.COM

FREE SUBSCRIPTION TO DI NEWSLETTER

Receive free unpublished articles by top DI authors, exclusive
discounts, and free downloads from our best and newest books.
Visit www.destinyimage.com to subscribe.

Write to: Destiny Image
              P.O. Box 310
              Shippensburg, PA 17257-0310

Call: 1-800-722-6774

Email: orders@destinyimage.com

For a complete list of our titles or to place an order
online, visit www.destinyimage.com.

FIND US ON FACEBOOK OR FOLLOW US ON TWITTER.

www.facebook.com/destinyimage   facebook
www.twitter.com/destinyimage   twitter